The Renewal of Anglicanism

By the same author

Iustitia Dei: A History of the Christian Doctrine of Justification

Luther's Theology of the Cross

The Intellectual Origins of the European Reformation

The Making of Modern German Christology

Editor, *The Blackwell Encyclopedia of Modern Christian Thought*

The Renewal

of

Anglicanism

Alister E. McGrath

MOREHOUSE PUBLISHING
Harrisburg, PA

Morehouse Publishing
P.O. Box 1321
Harrisburg, PA 17105

Library of Congress Cataloging-in-Publication Data:
McGrath, Alister E., 1953-
    The renewal of anglicanism / Alister E. McGrath.
        p.   cm.
    Includes bibliographical references and index.
    ISBN 0-8192-1612-7 (pbk.)
    1. Anglican Communion.   2. Church renewal.   I. Title.
BX5005.M447   1993
283—dc20   93-35681
                                                                            CIP

Printed in the United States of America
by
BSC LITHO

Contents

Foreword

There are few things, if any, that I long more to see than the renewal of Anglicanism, so I was happy indeed to be invited to write a foreword to this book. I was not born into Anglicanism, but came in by deliberate choice after long consideration, having grown up and even having done my theological training and served in the ministry of another theological tradition. One does not take such a drastic step without believing that there are good reasons for it. So I came into the Anglican Communion with all the zeal of a convert, and now, after thirty years as an Anglican, I have no doubt that I made the right choice. Converts are often more appreciative of the virtues of the tradition which they enter than those who were brought up in it, and for whom familiarity has dulled perception of its merits. At the same time, I think I have now been long enough in the Anglican Communion to have got beyond uncritical admiration, and to realize how deep is the need for a new infusion of vitality. At present, Anglicanism is in a state of disarray. Not only is it suffering from deep internal divisions; the older branches of the communion in Europe and North America are suffering a catastrophic decline in numbers.

The early chapters of Dr. McGrath's book are diagnostic. He believes that since the 1960s, when some theologians were proclaiming the "death of God" and much of their teaching was either negative or insipid, the Anglican churches in the West have been declining into a weariness or even a sickness. But he is not prepared to accept this situation lying down, as if increasing secularism is an inexorable fate. Rather, he sees the situation as a challenge to renewal and evangelism, and he believes that the Anglican heritage has much that enables the challenge to be met.

One of his recommendations is that we should seek to

1

reconstruct the *via media*. That "middle way" was meant to be a path of reconciliation for the diverse groups who were to be held together in the post-Elizabethan Church of England. But today it has become a dividing line between hostile parties. On the one side are the "liberals" who, in Dr. McGrath's view, are in fact often most illiberal and unwilling to allow any position other than their own. On the other side are conservatives, both catholic and evangelical, but lumped together by the liberals under the derogatory label of "fundamentalists." This term was first used in the United States about eighty years ago, and at that time had a fairly definite meaning. But it has now become a vague term of abuse. So perhaps our first step must be for churchpeople of all shades within Anglicanism to learn a new respect for one another, and to ensure that no group is marginalized.

A second step is to renew our roots. It is pointed out that two great moments of Anglican renewal in the past were brought about by going back to the roots. In the sixteenth-century Reformation, our leaders went back to retrieve the authentic gospel of the New Testament. In the Oxford Movement of three centuries later, a new group of leaders brought to light again the catholic basis of Anglicanism and prepared the way for the vigorous advances of the nineteenth century. So what is to be done? Dr. McGrath believes that a special responsibility and opportunity lies with our theological colleges or seminaries. But he visualizes them as extending their educational ministry to the whole church, laypeople as well as clerics and clerics-to-be.

I cannot always go along with Dr McGrath's ideas – for example, I am more doubtful than he is about the merits of what is called "postliberal" theology. But perhaps it is ungracious for me even to utter this mild *caveat*, for the book, coming as it does from a still young theologian, inspires new hope for the future of Anglicanism. Indeed, this book is in itself the beginning of the renewal, a first step in the thinking, talking and action that under God will bring new life to his people.

John Macquarrie

Introduction

There's a story behind every book. This one had its origins in late 1992, when Bishop Michael Marshall asked me to give an address on "The Renewal of Anglican Theology" at the Anglican Institute in Colorado Springs in the autumn of 1993. The idea attracted me, not least because it resonated with the growing interest in Anglican thought among many younger theologians, and my own personal concern for the church I have served as an ordained minister for the last thirteen years. A series of seminars organized in 1988–89 by the faculty of theology of Oxford University, focusing on aspects of Anglican theology in celebration of the centenary of *Lux Mundi*, had earlier provided me with some stimulus to reflection on such themes.[1]

I had long felt that a fresh approach is needed if Anglicanism in the West is to rediscover its purpose and potential. Like many younger Anglican theologians throughout the Western world, I considered that the new focus on evangelism within Anglicanism, coupled with the growing appreciation of the importance of the developing churches within the Anglican Communion, held the key to the renewal of Western Anglican theology. As both a theologian and an Anglican, I approached the subject with some enthusiasm.

However, as I talked with colleagues about the book and devoured the considerable literature devoted to the subject, I began to realize that a book could not at present be written on this theme. The renewal of Anglican *theology* depends on the prior renewal of *Anglicanism*. It is not theology that brings a church into being. Theology is what erupts from a self-confident and reflective community of faith, in possession of a vision of why it exists and what it proposes to do. It is the expression, not the cause, of that

3

vision. As Ninian Smart has perceptively pointed out, "doing theology, in the proper sense, is articulating a faith."[2] If there is no faith to articulate, theology has nothing to convey or express. Theology may help the community of faith to judge, reformulate, contextualize, and better articulate its vision – but it cannot create that vision in the first place. There is a real danger that Anglican theology may become little more than the guardian of the ideas of a dying church, which has lost its sense of purpose and direction in a changing and confusing world. A vibrant tradition of theological reflection is the outcome, rather than the cause, of a dynamic community of faith.

In the 1960s, the "Death of God" controversy erupted. Much attention was paid to its ideas, but too little to the spiritual vacuum and lack of religious vitality within the mainline churches which seem to have occasioned it. David Jenkins, now bishop of Durham, pointed this out forcefully at the time:

> While most of the philosophy and theology contained in the "Death of God" literature seems to be very second-rate or worse, it is very necessary to reflect on how absolutely deadly must have been the experience which the writers of this literature must have had, both in the worshipping and in the theological lives of their churches. For example, the God whose death is proclaimed in Thomas Altizer's *The Gospel of Christian Atheism* is a very sick God indeed. But someone must have given him this idea of God. The evidence suggests that it comes from a very sick church.[3]

A tired and dull church makes for a wearisome and unfocused theology. Yet a church with a sense of purpose and identity might well give rise to some exciting thinking. The renewal of Anglican theology is clearly linked with the spiritual and intellectual revitalization of Anglicanism as a whole, and cannot be isolated from this wider context.

Some Anglican writers spill much ink exploring what is distinctive about Anglicanism. There would seem to be little point in defending or rejoicing in the "distinctiveness" of Anglicanism,

4

if Anglicanism turns out merely to be distinctly dead. I can see little point it identifying what is distinctive about a Christian tradition, unless that tradition is characterized by a dynamism and vitality which would make others wish to imitate it. Unless Anglicanism renews itself, its distinctive ideas and ethos may well be studied only by others who wish to avoid our mistakes. The very fact that Anglicanism is so obviously inneed of renewal must mean taking the risk that some distinctive aspects of the Anglican ethos are actually *wrong*, and have contributed to our present sorry state. A church which refuses to acknowledge, let alone to learn from, its mistakes cannot expect to survive long in the harsh world of the future.

To write a book entitled "The Renewal of Anglicanism" is to suggest that Anglicanism needs renewal, that it can be renewed, and that it is worth renewing in the first place. It is quite likely that there will be some who will disagree with one or all of these suggestions. It may even be necessary to invite some readers to enter into a willing suspension of disbelief. However, I happen to believe that they are all merited, and that the future of the universal church will be enhanced and enriched by the presence of a renewed and resurgent Anglicanism.

Yet I have to confess a degree of hesitation over so many of the solutions offered by well-meaning Anglican apologists to the problems of today. Much has been written, and some of the best of it by Anglicans, on the impact of secularization upon Western culture and its implications for Christianity.[4] Yet many Western Anglicans seem to possess a feeling that the cultural tide must one day turn to reward those who wait patiently for its shift, pathetically clasping their volumes of Richard Hooker as they watch. Perhaps one of the most influential images to control English thinking on this theme is due to Matthew Arnold, who used the evocative image of the ebbing of the tide on Dover Beach as a symbol of the gradual loss of faith in Victorian England.

The sea of faith
Was once, too, at the full, and round earth's shore

5

Lay like the folds of a bright girdle furled.
But now I only hear
Its melancholy, long, withdrawing roar.[5]

Some suggest that we ought to hang around creatively, waiting for the tide to turn – as it must, given Arnold's analogy. Yet in the first place, such a passive approach is not worthy of Anglicanism. One cannot behave like an inverted Canute, in the hope that what appears to be a receding tide might return. Renewal may well mean a painful process of self-examination, in which many cherished ideas and approaches of the past are set to one side as redundant and unhelpful. It may mean taking risks, stepping out of the safety of the settled Anglican ethos that has emerged within the West, and exploring approaches that are new to Western Anglicanism, even if they have become the common currency in Anglicanism in Africa and Asia. We cannot afford to wait for a sea change that may never happen. Rather, we must seek out the opportunities for growth and renewal, wherever they may lie.

In the second place, it would seem that the analogy is, in one respect, flawed. Arnold's image of the "eternal note of sadness" evoked by the withdrawing tide is powerful and poetic and has captured the imagination of many.[6] It is also, quite frankly, more than a little shallow, betrayed by an unconscious late nineteenth-century Eurocentrism which extrapolates to the global from the local situation.[7] It is absurd to talk about faith "being at its full . . . round earth's shore," when Christianity had yet to make significant inroads in southern Africa, Asia, or even the Western seaboard of North America. At the time at which Arnold was writing, Christianity was geographically restricted, even if a combination of poetic license and an unconscious prioritization of the English situation may have clouded his judgment in this respect. Faith may indeed have been ebbing in Victorian England; it was, however, only on the point of being born in southern Africa and east Asia, as Christianity – including Anglicanism – prepared to expand into new arenas. Arnold's lament for the demise of faith in Western Europe is actually an anticipation of a future global change of balance within Christianity, as a movement whose powerhouses once centered on Western Europe began to shift to southern Africa and Asia.

Such shifts have taken place before in the long history of Christianity, most notably during the Dark Ages, as the center of gravity of Christian life and thought gradually moved from the Mediterranean world to Western Europe. What to one observer, located in the south-eastern Mediterranean, might seem like the ebbing of faith would seem to another, located in Western Europe, as the dawn of a new age of faith.[8] A Western perspective has dominated Anglican self-perception, with the result that our attention has focused on our own experience of a faith that is faltering. But there are other perspectives; indeed, those other perspectives are increasingly coming to represent the majority position within Anglicanism, especially in Asia and Africa. And that perspective is of advancement, increasing confidence, and a growing concern for the lack of vitality of faith and what appears to be a tendency to capitulate to secular pressures in the former heartlands of Anglicanism – in other words, in the West.

Our thinking on the future of faith must not be controlled by a single image, especially one so ethnocentric and theologically unsubstantiated as Arnold's. Others are available. One such image deployed recently by some Australian writers, surveying the possibilities for church growth in that region, caught my attention a few years ago. Although decidedly less poetic than Matthew Arnold's powerful image of the ebbing tide on Dover Beach, it probably has considerably greater cultural warrant and theological credibility.

Once upon a time there was a mighty river. It flowed gracefully and eloquently across the landscape. Along its banks it gave life and sustenance to the tribes of Aboriginal Australians who camped by it. For many generations this river was a central focus for life. Then, gradually, the river ceased to flow, becoming a stagnant pool. With the heat of summer, it started to dry up. Around the banks of the disappearing symbol of their security, the people watched aghast. What

7

could be happening to them? By the dried up river-bed many sat, waiting for the river to flow once more. Yet others thought to look around, and discovered that the river was not gone. Still flowing, it had simply changed course upstream, creating a billabong on the curve at which they sat.[9]

Has God's life-giving Spirit moved on in new directions, bidding us to follow? Instead of waiting for the billabong to refill, we might well do better to seek and follow the new paths in which God is at work in his church throughout the world. Instead of sitting morosely on Dover Beach waiting for the tide to turn, we should be seeking the new directions in which God may be leading his churches as we prepare to enter the new millennium. And both the stimulus for such reflection and the paradigms upon which it may be based are increasingly due to Anglicanism in the developing regions of the world. Our hopes for renewal may well rest upon emulating the dynamism of Asian dioceses such as Sabah and Singapore.

Many will, however, feel that to speak of a "renewed Anglicanism" is to lapse into the crude triumphalism and imperialism that have been so distressing a feature of Anglican apologetics in the past. Personally, I cringe on reading certain older works lauding the "genius of Anglicanism" which often seem depressingly like ecclesiastical renditions of "Rule Britannia." In common with most younger Anglicans, I have no interest in the justification of Anglicanism upon the grounds of tradition or sentiment. There is no place in the kingdom of God for a church whose credentials rest solely upon past distinction, rather than present-day relevance. Nevertheless, I believe that Anglicanism has a continuing role to play in global Christianity, not on account of its historical origins or alleged past greatness, but on account of its present form and content, and the shared anticipations of its future. It is a movement that is profoundly worthy of renewing, on account of its potential contribution to the well-being and mission of the body of Christ throughout the world. My own commitment to Anglicanism arises from a greater commitment to the future of global Christianity, linked to a conviction that Anglicanism has a merited and distinctive place in that future.

Yet it is not adequate merely to speak of "renewal" or "growth." Too often, the bright ideas and radical innovations of enthusiastic theologians turn out to have value, if they have any value at all, only in the short term. As the marked ambivalence within Anglican circles recently toward the legacy of the 1960s has made quite clear, what seemed to be a good idea to one generation can easily become an embarrassing liability to another. As Thomas C. Oden, a 1960s break-with-roots radical turned 1980s return-to-roots radical, pointed out, the church has become wearied by "a long parade of novelties that promised the moon and delivered green cheese . . . Contemporary preaching, liturgics and pastoral care are strewn with the wreckage of such fantasies."[10] We can do without these flashes in the Anglican pan, which offer quick fixes without addressing the real issues troubling Anglicanism at the moment – quick fixes, it turns out, without any real grounding in the Christian tradition or sustained experience of pastoral ministry. It is vital to develop a strategy for sustainable renewal on the basis of assumptions that are likely to retain their credibility in the longer term. This will inevitably mean a change in attitudes and expectations within Western Anglicanism, especially within institutions of theological education responsible for the intellectual, spiritual and pastoral equipping of the Anglican leaders of the future. Renewal will mean changes at the structural level, as a church that has become used to maintenance becomes orientated toward mission. Yet there are ample indications that there is an openness towards such reconsideration at every level of Anglicanism today.

Perhaps my judgment is flawed. Perhaps Anglicanism will turn out to have little to offer the universal church other than the platitudes of our urbane past, or the failed remedies of our liberal Western yesteryears. Sadly, that will probably spell the end of Anglicanism in the West; it will not, however, mean its demise elsewhere. This little book is a plea that this dereliction of our heritage must not be allowed to happen, and an expression of the hope that both Western Christianity and the universal church will be enriched by the continuing presence of an Anglicanism within its ranks which is as self-confident as it is self-critical.

This book is not a list of practical recommendations. I have little time for the "press-these-buttons-and-things-will-get-better" school of thought. The issues that attend the renewal of Anglicanism are too complex to be handled in this way. Rather, I have been concerned to explore what has happened recently in Anglicanism, and how this might have a bearing on the future renewal of that church in the West. Above all, I have been concerned to stress the importance of rediscovering a sense of purpose, instead of aimlessly plodding along from one issue to another, wondering what will happen next. Anglicanism needs to make its own future, instead of just allowing things – usually rather nasty things – to happen to it.

In writing this book, I have incurred a debt too great to acknowledge, let alone to repay, to many Anglican colleagues over the last three years, especially in Oxford and London, but also in Chicago, Los Angeles, Melbourne, Sydney, and Vancouver. Yet curiously, the stimulus to renew Anglicanism has also come from outside its ranks. One of the greatest delights in talking through the themes of this book with my non-Anglican friends has been the enthusiasm with which they responded to the vision of a renewed Anglicanism. I had thought they might be threatened by this possibility. Far from it. Their response has typically been "If Anglicanism can renew itself, then so can we." As those colleagues pointed out, many of the approaches explored in this work can easily be adapted to non-Anglican contexts. So, despite its many inadequacies, this little book is offered as a contribution to the worldwide renewal of the church of Jesus Christ, as it prepares to face the third, and perhaps the most challenging to date, millennium of its existence.

Alister McGrath   Oxford, Pentecost 1993

1

Anglicanism in Transition

Anglicanism is a glorious accident of history – a serendipity. It emerged from the world of political compromise of the sixteenth century, in which nations that had been broken and bruised by the turmoil of the Reformation sought to restore order to their churches, while responding to the genuine pressures which had unleashed such a wave of unrest. One such local development took place in England, as a harassed monarch looked for ways to achieve a workable middle way that would find acceptance among both traditional catholics and those who had been deeply influenced by the ideas of Luther and Calvin.

By international standards, England was then a backwater. It lacked the political, military, cultural and economic muscle power enjoyed by others on the continent of Europe. That would come later. This "Settlement of Religion" was a purely local arrangement, finely tuned to the English situation. England had lost its former possessions in Europe; it was now little more than the southern region of an island off the European mainland. Yet, perhaps more by accident than design, Elizabeth I arrived at a "Settlement of Religion" that would provide a framework for the emergence of a distinctive approach to Christianity.[1] Perhaps its merits were glimpsed dimly at that early stage in its development; as time progressed, however, they became increasingly apparent.

Through a complex pattern of historical development, conditioned by local, regional, and international factors, Anglicanism began to assume its familiar shape, ethos, and outlook.[2]

Anglicanism, then, is an historical contingency – but an historical contingency which, in the last two centuries, has proved to possess qualities that the modern church happens to need rather badly. William Temple identifies the distinctive features of that ethos as follows:

> Our special character and, as we believe, our peculiar contribution to the Universal Church, arises from the fact that, owing to historical circumstances, we have been enabled to combine in one fellowship the traditional faith and order of the catholic church with that immediacy of approach to God through Christ to which the evangelical churches especially bear witness, and freedom of intellectual inquiry, whereby the correlation of the Christian revelation and advancing knowledge is constantly effected.[3]

Note that Temple does not provide a definition or theological justification of Anglicanism. Rather, he is concerned to identify the distinctive shape of the movement, and the particular strengths and gifts that it might make available to the church as a whole.

Perhaps an awareness of these localized historical origins has prevented Anglicans from committing the ultimate act of theological arrogance and declaring that Anglicanism is *the* universal church or is somehow a definitive form of Christianity. One of the most attractive and winsome features of recent Anglican writings has been an informed awareness that the movement is part of a greater movement, with no particular pretensions to global domination.[4] As William Temple put it, Anglicanism has a *contribution* to make to the universal church. A theology of Christian interdependence and mutual enrichment nestles within this approach, which is prepared to concede that Anglicanism has no claim to *being* the universal church, yet wishes to enrich and contribute to that greater whole.

Yet Anglicanism is changing. Adaptation is here to be seen as a sign of life. Some might wish to petrify Anglicanism, preserving, like a fly trapped in amber, the particular religious ethos of Caroline or Victorian England and treating this as normative for all time. Yet this work is written in the full knowledge that Anglicanism has changed radically since the halcyon days of the English Reformation, the Caroline Divines and the Oxford Movement (to name three moments in English history regarded as normative by some Anglicans). Much of that change is very recent, to be dated within the last three decades; some is more recent still. In what follows, I shall note four such changes, and provide a brief assessment of their significance for Anglicanism worldwide.

The Enlightenment Is Over

At some point around 1750, a major shift began to take place in Western Europe and North America. The period in question, known as the "Enlightenment," was destined to have a major impact on Christianity in those regions.[5] The movement asserted the omnicompetence of human reason. Reason, it was argued, was capable of telling us everything we needed to know about God and morality. The idea of some kind of supernatural revelation was dismissed as an irrelevance. Jesus Christ was just one of many religious teachers, who told us things that anyone with a degree of common sense could have told us anyway. Reason reigned supreme.

This approach was clearly inconsistent with the New Testament picture of Christ as redeemer and savior. This problem was soon disposed of. According to rationalist writers, the New Testament represented a deliberate distortion of Jesus. The gospels tried to rewrite history. Jesus was a wandering preacher, whose followers expected great things of him. Unfortunately, he was executed in a particularly degrading and humiliating manner. Unable to accept this shameful end to Jesus' career, his disciples invented a happier ending: Jesus was raised from the dead. The resurrection was thus pure invention – an invention that could, according to such rationalist writers, be exposed by going back behind the New

13

Testament to rediscover the real "Jesus of history."[6]

The theory had great appeal, with its cloak-and-dagger approach and its bold claim to discredit Christianity. It had the David-and-Goliath angle loved by journalists. Imagine a humble honest scholar, passionately seeking after the truth, bringing the massive edifice of Christianity tumbling to the ground! The same theory has appeared many times since then, with publishers and television producers outdoing each other in hyping up the results. In the meantime, largely unnoticed, real New Testament scholarship has plodded on patiently in the background.[7] Its results are far less exciting to a largely secular Western world looking for an instant fix and a good reason to dismiss Christianity, yet far more reliable.

The regions of the world in which the Enlightenment gained its greatest influence (western Europe and North America) were Christian. As a result, it is Christianity, of all the world's religions, that was subjected to the most devastating and penetrating criticisms at the hands of this aggressive rationalism. The criticisms directed against Christianity could equally have been directed against, for example, Judaism or Islam; with rare exceptions, they were not. The result of this frontal assault was to create something approaching a siege mentality within sections of Christianity.

Some welcomed this development, regarding it as a permanent change in human culture. The contributors to *The Myth of God Incarnate* (1977) seem to have regarded the Enlightenment as something that was given and fixed for all time. It was here, and it was right. For example, Leslie Houlden argued that we have no option but to accept the rationalist outlook of the Enlightenment and restructure our Christian thinking accordingly. "We must accept our lot, bequeathed to us by the Enlightenment, and make the most of it."[8] Yet even as Houlden was writing, the Enlightenment world-view was dying. What was once thought to be a universal worldview was increasingly recognized to be a purely Western phenomenon, which Western academics and politicians sought to impose on others.

The rise of the movement that is now generally known as "postmodernism" throughout the Western world is a direct result of both the collapse of this confidence in reason and a more general disillusionment with the so-called "modern" world.[9] Postmodernism is the intellectual movement which proclaims that, in the first place, the Enlightenment rested on fraudulent intellectual foundations (such as the belief in the omnicompetence of human reason), and in the second, it ushered in some of the most horrific events in human history – such as the Stalinist purges and the Nazi extermination camps.[10] The new cultural mood that developed in the 1980s rebelled against the Enlightenment. Who wanted anything to do with an intellectually dubious movement that had given rise to the Nazi holocaust and the Stalinist purges?

There has thus been a general collapse of confidence in the Enlightenment trust in the power of reason to provide foundations for a universally valid knowledge of the world, including God. Reason fails to deliver a morality suited to the real world in which we live. And with this collapse of confidence in universal and necessary criteria of truth, relativism and pluralism have flourished. In the 1880s, Nietzsche declared, somewhat prematurely as it turned out, that "God is dead!" More recently, it is the death of the Enlightenment which is being proclaimed. It remains far from clear what will replace it. But what is clear is that the claustrophobic and restrictive straitjacket placed upon Western Christianity by rationalism has gone. In the space of the last two decades, there has been a major cultural shift in Western society, that opens up new opportunities for the churches. Anglicanism is well placed to benefit from this development.

One reason for this is the international character of Anglicanism. During the last century, Anglicanism has gained in strength considerably in regions of the world in which the Enlightenment has had minimal impact – such as sub-Saharan Africa. As Western theology begins to recollect its roots again, rediscovering ideas and approaches that the cultural pressures of the Enlightenment forced to the theological margins, it can listen to and learn from the dynamic living traditions of Anglican communities that have retained those ideas and approaches.

An excellent example is provided by the new interest in *narrative*, unquestionably one of the most important developments in modern theology. With the widespread rejection of the Enlightenment idea of "universal rationality," there has been new interest in returning to the "story-based world" of Scripture.[11] Yet such approaches to the reading and understanding of Scripture are, and have been, typical of African cultures, in which a dynamic and interactive mode of reading Scripture has developed. Western Anglicanism could do far worse than listen to their story.

The Impact of African and Asian Anglicanism

Much has been written about the virtues of a "universal" church, that transcends the limits of culture and history. Yet "universal" can all too often mean homeless. An attempt to belong everywhere is often flawed by an obstinate and radical failure to belong *anywhere*. Esperanto has pretensions to being a universal language. Yet it is known by an insignificant number of people, is the first and natural language of none, has given rise to no literature, and has shaped no culture. It is an artificial construction whose claims to universality are overshadowed by its failure to have taken root anywhere.

Anglicanism represents an attempt to ground the Christian vision in a specific culture, at a specific time. Its distinctive features may be argued to lie in its application of the gospel to a specific historical situation – England, and subsequently the British colonies. Louis Weil states this point carefully:

The gospel in Anglicanism is . . . one facet in a vast mosaic. In its essentials, it corresponds to the gospel as it has been proclaimed and believed all over the world. Yet it is also characterized by its particularity as an experience of God's saving work in particular cultures, and is shaped by the insights and limitations of persons who were themselves seeking to live the gospel within a particular context.[12]

16

That context was initially sixteenth-century England. Given that Anglicanism was the established church in England, it was perhaps inevitable that the expansion of British influence around the world, especially during the nineteenth century, would be accompanied by an extension of Anglicanism. By the end of the first decade of the twentieth century, Anglicanism could easily be caricatured as little more than the British Empire at prayer. (The inconvenient exception to this rule was the United States; this could be accommodated by English apologists, however, on the assumption that it was simply a rebellious British colony that had the good sense to retain Anglicanism, even if it rejected the British *imperium* which traditionally accompanied it.) That caricature is now hopelessly outdated, losing whatever validity it may once have possessed; the establishment of Anglican provinces in Zaire (a former Belgian colony) and Korea (where the colonial power was Japan) points to the growing impact of Anglicanism outside both the English-speaking world and the former British Empire.

Yet the taint of "Englishness" remains. The result of this has been unfortunate but, happily, not irreversible. Too often in the past international Anglicanism has been seen as a safe haven for expatriate Brits in alien cultures or a gathering point for culturally alienated Anglophiles with a taste for Trollopian characters or Tudor church music. The result is that Anglicanism runs the risk of becoming an Anglo-Saxon ghetto in the West, a problem especially evident in some parts of Australia. The failure of Anglicanism to establish itself properly in the Riverina area of New South Wales has been put down to the uncritical and inappropriate application of English styles of ministry in a context that demanded the development of local approaches.[13] Even in Sydney, perhaps the most successful Anglican diocese in this region in terms of its outreach, Anglicanism continues to run the risk of being an Anglo-Saxon enclave in the midst of a multicultural situation.[14] The near-total failure of Anglicanism to establish itself in continental Europe is also an important consideration in this respect. Happily, the Anglican experience in Africa and Asia has shown how this need not be the case;

17

nevertheless, serious questions remain about the universality of Anglicanism in the West.

In an important critique of Latin American liberation theology, Jürgen Moltmann made the point that there was little about the movement that was demonstrably Latin American. "One reads more about the sociological theories of others, namely Western sociologists, than about the history of the life and suffering of Latin American people."[15] And while I have no intention of belittling the sacrifices and efforts of earlier generations of Anglican missionaries and bishops, I cannot fail to point out how there was often a shocking failure to appreciate the sensitivities and values of the cultural contexts in which they sought to establish Anglicanism. Too often, Christianity and middle-class English cultural values got muddled up. The word "heathen" was often used indiscriminately to mean "non-European" or "strange." Bolaji Idowu writes of the consequences of this colonialist attitude for his native Nigeria:

> If, at the beginning, anyone had had enough vision to suggest that while accepting Christianity, Nigerians did not need to throw away what was good and valuable in their own culture, such a person would have been accused of rank "heathenism" by the European religious educators whose set purpose was to exterminate as of the Devil anything that had no meaning for them.[16]

A substantial part of the agenda of Christian writers throughout the non-Western world has been the liberation of Christianity from its Western matrix. Uganda and India, in different ways, represent cases in point.[17] The basic issue here is that of constructing a "local theology," in which the "seed of faith is allowed to interact with the native soil, leading to a new flowering of Christianity, faithful both to the local culture and to the apostolic faith."[18]

This strongly European ethnocentrism has a further consequence, that needs to be addressed. It is not simply that early Anglican missionaries assumed that their British values and approaches were intrinsically correct; they also ignored or suppressed the cultural and social roots of those to whom they ministered. The most sensitive exploration of this issue that I have encountered is in the writings of the Ghanaian author Kwame Bediako. Bediako points out how African Christians were often put in the intolerable position of being obliged to turn their backs on their own traditions and culture and rely on a borrowed European heritage.[19] This served to reinforce the perception that Christianity was culturally alien to Africa – a perception that was particularly acute in the case of Anglicanism, which retained ample outward manifestations of its English origins (for example, the virtually universal use of the Book of Common Prayer until the Second World War). The rapid recent growth of African independent churches, which make extensive use of local African traditions and values within a Christian context, is an indication of the extent of the reaction against such cultural suppression.[20]

The dominance of Western Anglicanism, and more specifically *English* Anglicanism, probably ended about 1980. If this fact has not been universally conceded, it is largely on account of its having been unintentionally concealed by the perceived academic superiority of the West. The continuing literary output of Western publishing houses and the dominance of Western academics in global discussions of issues of religion and theology mask the shift away from the traditional zones of strength of Anglicanism. Timothy E. Yates notes this point in a recent essay:

> Much of the liveliest Anglican life exists in Africa south of the Sahara, in Asia and in Latin America. These voices will claim a hearing increasingly in Anglican consultations and may act as a healthy corrective to the Anglicanism of the comparatively settled, wealthy and arid north, arid in the view of many of these communities because of what is perceived as an over-intellectualized theological tradition and a weakened spirituality.[21]

To give one outstanding example of this point: the call at the 1988 Lambeth Conference for a renewed commitment to evangelism came from African church leaders, such as Bishop Dinis Sengulane of Lebombo, Mozambique. The Lambeth declaration that "evangelism is the primary task given to the church"[22] is widely regarded as a direct consequence of the growing presence and power of the African churches and their increasing impatience with the spiritual complacency of their Western brothers and sisters.[23] This development is in itself of considerable importance, and requires further discussion.

A New Emphasis on Evangelism

Traditionally, Anglican understandings of the nature of the church have been grounded on the presumption that the church is situated within a largely settled Christian context and is thus primarily concerned with pastoral care and teaching. The dominance of this model within the Western tradition can be seen in the written form of the Japanese term for church, *kyōkai*, where the two characters (*kanji*) used to represent the term have the natural meaning of "a teaching organization," representing the dominant ecclesiology of the nineteenth-century Western missionaries. Yet that settled Christian situation is not typical of global Anglicanism. The dominance of this model of the church is due to the historical predominance of Western churches within Anglicanism. But that period of dominance is over. As power and growth shift to African, Asian, and Latin American churches, so the idea of proclamation and mission have come to assume increased prominence within Anglican conceptions of the church.

One of the major developments in Western culture within the last thirty years has been massive immigration into its cities, especially from Asia. Whether one looks at London, Toronto, Vancouver, Los Angeles, San Diego, Sydney, or Melbourne, the same pattern emerges. There is a growing presence of non-Christian religions in regions that hitherto might have regarded themselves as nominally Christian. The result has been unequivocal: the same conditions faced by Anglicans in Africa and Asia have now arisen in many areas of the West. Western Anglicans, who up to this point could, with varying degrees of credibility, have regarded their societies as nominally Christian, requiring pastoral care and social justice, are now having to adjust to the emergence of a missionary situation directly paralleling those faced by Anglicans elsewhere in the world.

Many Western Anglicans remain isolated from this development. Clergy working in rural areas of south-western England, or the deep south of Ireland, might well feel totally unable to identify with the cultural shifts just noted. But they are a major feature of life in most modern Western cities and give every indication of becoming more widespread as time passes. Western forms of Anglicanism, accustomed to dealing with settled geographical patterns of religious affiliations, are not especially well placed to cope with these developments, often regarding them with a mixture of mild amusement, paternalism, and panic. Yet African and Asian Anglicans have been confronted with this pattern of religious affiliation since Anglicanism became established in their regions. As a result, they have developed techniques and attitudes for coping with them – attitudes and techniques that Western Anglicanism needs to evaluate and assimilate as a matter of urgency. It is no longer possible for Western Anglicanism to entrust its future to a pastoral understanding of the church that reflects the social conditions of sixteenth-century England. Anglicans in regions such as Kenya and Uganda, Sabah and Singapore, have developed approaches to mission and ministry that the Western church cannot afford to ignore, least of all on the basis of the patronizing assumption that "we in the West know better."

The growing influence of African and Asian Anglicanism and the increased relevance of its agenda to Anglicanism in the West was evident at the 1988 Lambeth Conference. A direct result of this has been explicit statement by that conference to the effect that the primary task of the church is now to be seen as *evangelism* – that is, "a dynamic missionary emphasis going beyond care and nurture to proclamation and service."[24] This new direction in Anglican ecclesiology has taken many by surprise. For example, the magisterial collection of essays *The Study of Anglicanism*, which appeared in 1988 in preparation for the Lambeth

21

Conference, does not so much as mention "evangelism" in its index, although the "Eton College case" merits a generous three mentions near the place where one might expect to find such reference.

The 1988 Lambeth Conference gave Anglicanism a new sense of direction and purpose through its firm long-term commitment to evangelism throughout the communion. In an increasingly secular age, evangelism is coming to be seen as of decisive importance in reaching out beyond the bounds of the church and bringing women and men the good news of Jesus Christ. Once more, the 1988 Lambeth Conference recognized the urgency of this situation and pointed to the important role models available for the Western churches in their more vibrant sister churches in Africa, Asia, and Latin America.

> Though there are notable exceptions, the dominant model of the church within the Anglican Communion is a pastoral one. Emphasis in all aspects of the church's life tends to be placed upon care and nurture, rather than proclamation and service. The pressing needs of today's world demand that there be a massive shift to a "mission" orientation throughout the communion . . . This is beginning to happen in many parts of Africa, Asia and Latin America.[25]

There is a growing realization, even within the depths of a frequently rather complacent church establishment, that the future existence and well-being of the churches depends on a determined and principled effort to proclaim the gospel.

There are still those within Anglicanism, especially in the United Kingdom and North America, who resist this development and equate evangelism with "Christian imperialism." These attitudes, that in the past have been especially associated with the World Council of Churches, are totally unfounded; they rest upon dangerously superficial understandings of the nature of the gospel in general, and evangelism in particular. Evangelism is not based on an imperialist craving to dominate the world, but on a longing to *share* the good news of God with a world that sorely needs hope and forgiveness. It is something that springs from the deepest feelings of love and a heartfelt desire to share something that it would be selfish and irresponsible to keep to oneself. The World Council of Churches, apparently blinded by its ability to see things only in terms of "power" and "domination," has lost sight of a central theme of the Christian gospel.

The World Council of Churches has often been criticized for its uncritical use of the language and categories of Marxism, where those of Christianity might seem more appropriate. The use of the term "imperialism" is a case in point. The term first passed into general use through the writings of V. I. Lenin, especially his 1916 pamphlet *Imperialism: The Highest Stage of Capitalism*.[26] A close reading of this pamphlet suggests that Lenin tended to think of imperialism primarily in economic terms. However Karl Kautsky (1854–1938), the leading Marxist thinker of the Second International, defined imperialism more generally, in terms of the relationship between the advanced and underdeveloped nations, especially the political domination of underdeveloped countries by developed nations such as Britain and the United States.

The unreflective use of the term "imperialism" to refer to evangelization appears to be grounded in the belief that Christian mission is merely the religious component of a general economic and political program of global domination by the West. The empirical evidence allows this assumption to be refuted. As the 1988 Lambeth Conference makes clear, evangelism is actually something to which the *underdeveloped* nations are calling the *developed* nations – a total inversion of the situation envisaged by the "evangelism-as-domination" school. The demand for increased priority to be given to evangelism came especially from the bishops of east Africa, with powerful support from the east Asian bishops; the greatest resistance to this suggestion appears to have come from the English and American bishops.

Happily, "evangelism as imperialism" attitudes now seem to belong firmly in the past. Those who publicly defend them today are often aware of being viewed as "old-fashioned" or "out of touch" by their increasingly unsympathetic audiences. There is now an increasing realization throughout the Christian West that the growing threat of secularization must be met. The Christian churches cannot rely on a legacy of cultural religiosity to ensure their continuing presence in the world. They must proclaim the profound attractiveness of faith to the world, in the full and confident expectation that the gospel is inherently attractive and relevant. As the distinguished Jesuit theologian Karl Rahner put it, "The possibility of winning new Christians from a milieu that has become unchristian is the sole living and convincing evidence that Christianity still has a real chance for the future."[27] The embargo placed by the mainline churches on evangelism is finally over.

Stephen Sykes, bishop of Ely and perhaps the most important recent analyst of the Anglican ethos, comments as follows on this shift, as he commends its vision and challenge:

> Realism and honesty compel us to admit that it is not self-evident for Anglicans to speak enthusiastically about evangelism . . . we have not been the most evangelistically minded of churches . . . But I believe this present decade is an opportunity for us corporately to study and acknowledge the strengths and weaknesses of our own tradition with a view to deepening our grasp upon evangelism, and do so without anxiety or over-cautious definition.[28]

Any account of Anglicanism since 1988 must give full weight to this development, as it must to the growing importance of the situations faced by Anglicanism outside its once-traditional homelands.

The Growth of Evangelicalism

Survey after survey demonstrates the same finding: evangelicalism is of growing importance to the worldwide church. Scarcely any part of the world has remained untouched by the global renaissance of evangelicalism. Even Latin America, traditionally regarded as a stronghold of Roman Catholicism, is now expected to become dominated by evangelicalism by the year 2025.[29] Anglicanism is no exception to this rule. It has been deeply affected, especially during the last two decades, by a resurgent evangelicalism within its ranks. The effect has perhaps been most noticeable in the Church of England; it is estimated that 55 percent of full-time ordinands in training for its ministry in 1993 are evangelicals.

Inevitably, the rapid global expansion of evangelicalism in the last two decades has raised considerable anxieties for many within Anglicanism, especially those of a more catholic outlook.[30] Yet Anglicanism is a living tradition, rather than a petrified fossil that bears only the marks of the past and has lost any ability to grow and develop in response to present conditions. It is a dynamic body, that is open to renewal and revitalization as an essential part of its communal life and development. During the 1830s, many more sceptical Anglicans regarded the Oxford Movement as an utterly un-Anglican development, that could only destroy the distinctiveness of the Church of England and move it closer to the Roman Catholic church. Its distinctive approach to worship was viewed with horror by some tender souls, who failed to appreciate that many ordinary parishioners genuinely found it to be helpful and conducive to the praise and adoration of God. This intense suspicion remained for some time. Happily, the Oxford Movement can now be seen for what it was – a renewing influence, bringing new life to the church and its worship.[31]

Those same charges are today being brought by some less perceptive critics against evangelicals. Yet evangelicalism is a force for renewal within today's Anglican Communion. As statistic after statistic reminds us, an Anglican church that is growing today is most likely to be evangelical in its orientation. Those who are so culturally conditioned that they are unable to worship save with the assistance of a full pipe organ and robed choir will naturally deplore the more liberated style of worship often associated with evangelicalism, that has proved so attractive and helpful to many – especially young people – who would otherwise have nothing to do with the church in any shape or form. Future historians are likely to view today's critics of Anglican evangelicalism with as little sympathy as yesterday's critics of Anglo-Catholicism.

In the Episcopal Church in the United States, evangelicalism has an especially important role to play, just as the Episcopal Church has an especially important role to play in relation to evangelicalism. Norman Pittenger is one of a number of recent Episcopalian writers who has stressed the "roominess" of American Anglicanism, and drawn attention to the fact that there is – and must be – room within that church for differing interpretations "providing that there is basic agreement about the basic things."

> Our ideal, however badly it may be realized, is that on essential matters there should be a basic unity; on inessential matters, and on interpretations of basic matters, a willingness to differ; in all things, a spirit of generosity and mutual understanding.[32]

Yet the same comprehensive ethos that demands that evangelicalism be welcomed and affirmed within the Episcopal Church also poses a challenge to evangelicalism itself. One of the less pleasant features of evangelicalism is its dogmatism, not simply in allegedly basic issues, but in certain matters of interpretation as well. The Episcopal Church has a long tradition of forcing Christians to learn to live with their differences. [33]

Tolerance of diversity in nonessentials is a lesson that evangelicals have to learn, not least by rediscovering the Reformation concept of *adiaphora* – a vital notion that seems to have escaped the attention of some evangelicals claiming to assume the mantle of the reformers in today's church. If Anglicanism needs evangelicalism's dynamism and vitality, evangelicalism needs Anglicanism's generosity and tolerance. The two are not incompatible! Perhaps the most obvious case illustrating the importance of this point is the recent controversy within the Southern Baptist Convention, that has so polarized the denomination. One of the most intelligent and insightful voices within that Convention is Timothy George, Dean of Beeson Divinity School at Samford University. In a privately published paper entitled *The Future for Theological Education Among*

Southern Baptists, George identifies precisely these issues as central to the future of such theological education. Noting the issues that divide this evangelical denomination – such as the role of women in ministry and charismatic renewal in the life of the church – George pleads for toleration in relation to marginalia, with a focus on agreement on the central issues. "If in this age of pluralism and every tub-sitting-on-its-own-bottom individualism, we cannot achieve consensus theology, perhaps we can at least learn to respect the integrity of individuals who in conscience do not agree with us."[34] As he observes, "a church which has become obsessed with the marginalia of the faith will soon find itself shipwrecked on the shoals of a fractured fellowship." Anglicanism, for all its faults and failings, provides a context in which agreement on essentials can exist alongside a debate over their interpretation and application, as well as allowing other marginal issues to remain creatively unresolved.

There is, however, a more serious point here, and one that increasingly demands attention. Evangelicalism is coming to dominate Christianity in the United States. Forms of American evangelicalism that are totally unsympathetic to the Anglican tradition are gaining ground and threaten to attract many out of all the mainline churches – not just the Episcopal Church – partly on account of a perceived hostility towards evangelicalism within those churches. The presence of evangelicalism within Anglicanism is a necessary check against this development and ensures that Anglicanism will, if anything, benefit from – rather than be seriously depleted by – the substantial growth in evangelicalism in North America. Rather than deplore this growth, those concerned for the future of Anglicanism would do better to encourage and nourish those evangelicals who are committed to Anglican outlooks and structures, thus ensuring that growth and renewal are channeled toward, rather than away from, Anglicanism. The situations in parts of New Zealand, Canada and the United States give cause for especial concern here; many young people are abandoning Anglicanism for evangelical churches on account of their perception (misguided, one hopes) that the former represents a rather unattractive and desiccated form of Christianity.

As I stressed above, there are strong indications that Anglican structures will prove themselves capable of checking the less acceptable features of evangelicalism. For all its dynamism, evangelicalism is perennially prone to lapse into rampant individualism, with no sense of "belonging in history" or of the common and shared aspects of Christian life. Anglicanism has proved to be a crucible in which evangelicalism is being refined, with its evangelistic fervor being channeled into stabilizing catholic structures. There is also a growing appreciation on the part of evangelicals for the importance of the Anglican pastoral and liturgical ethos. Space permits only one aspect of this to be illustrated. I have chosen the evangelical emphasis on evangelism to indicate how the Anglican ethos has proved to be increasingly welcome to evangelicals within the movement.

How do people come to faith? One of the most curious features of discussions of evangelism in Western churches, including Anglicanism, has been a reluctance to ask this obvious question. Yet the devising of appropriate apologetic and evangelistic strategies rests upon an understanding of how, as a matter of observable fact, individuals come to make the decision to become Christians. Such a survey was carried out recently in England, based on a sample of 500 people who had recently come to faith.[35] The results were highly significant. The most common routes to faith appear to be through personal friendships and the gradual personal assimilation of faith through church attendance. It is this latter that is of especial importance for Anglicanism. Why?

It is certainly true that many people come to faith in a dramatic and memorable manner, often making a decision to convert in response to an enormously powerful sermon, or an emotion-charged address at an evangelistic rally. Yet this, in common with every other route to faith, must not be allowed to become normative. How one person comes to faith must not be regarded as laying down how everyone else comes to faith. The simple observable fact seems to be that many people who come to faith do so by joining church congregations as "seekers" without necessarily wishing to be known as such. And, gradually, through a process of reflection and assimilation, they discover that they have accepted the Christian faith and regard themselves – as they in turn are regarded – as Christians.

An Anglican understanding of the church is entirely consistent with this proven and common route to faith. Indeed, more than that: it is ideally suited to it. Anglicanism has long been committed to an Augustinian, rather than a Donatist, view of the church – that is, to an understanding of the church as a "mixed body," including both believers and nonbelievers, rather than a "society of saints," from whose ranks those who have yet to come to faith, or whose faith is faltering or uncertain, are excluded as a matter of principle. Most Anglican clergy, in England as in other Western contexts, are well used to the fact that their congregations include seekers, hangers-on, and drifters, as well as committed believers. For the evangelical wing of the church in the past, this has been seen as an irritation. Now it is seen as a bonus and increasingly recognized by evangelical Anglicans as a vitally important point of contact between the church and the world, allowing evangelism to proceed quietly and discreetly, without putting "seekers" under pressure of any kind.

In a significant recent article, the leading Australian evangelical writer John Waterhouse argues that Australian evangelicalism may have lost its way. Surveying the movement, he comments:

> The only winner is, paradoxically, the Anglican church. With its tradition of not precipitously separating the wheat from the tares, or pressuring people into public commitments before they are ready, the tentative outsider is given time to grow into faith, while the long-term believer, burnt out by a negative church experience, is given time to lick his wounds.[36]

A separatist view of the church – favored by many non-Anglican evangelicals – carries with it the danger of imposing such doctrinal commitments upon church attendance that the mere attending of church can be seen as equivalent to a public Christian profession. It was this separatist view of the church was was so decisively

29

rejected by evangelical Anglicans in England at the historic confrontation between John R. W. Stott and Martin Lloyd-Jones in 1966 and subsequently affirmed at the National Evangelical Anglican Congress the following year. The more Anglican tradition thus affirmed (which corresponds to the Augustinian outlook of the mainstream Reformation) is that of assuming that the congregation will include both believers and unbelievers, and that attendance at church does not necessarily signify any profession of Christian faith.[37] As noted earlier, statistics suggest strongly that one of the most important routes by which many people (especially those over the age of 30) come to faith is through attending church, and gradually assimilating, accepting and responding to the gospel. A separatist ecclesiology, with its emphasis upon commitment and doctrinal purity, makes this proven route to faith highly problematic.

Anglicanism did not invent this approach to church membership on the basis of a realization that it would be conducive to church growth. It emerged through a combination of historical factors, many linked with the situation in which the Elizabethan church found itself in the 1560s. It is now an established feature of the Anglican ethos, that has proved itself to be highly effective at the pastoral and evangelistic levels. To put it bluntly: people do not generally feel threatened about the idea of attending an Anglican church. It is not seen as weird or bizarre. It is almost something *normal*. And while many would deplore this, wishing to see church attendance as a public expression of commitment, Anglicanism has always given people the benefit of the doubt.

As the drift back to church gains pace in the West, Anglicanism seems to be poised to be one of its chief beneficiaries. Evangelicals have noticed this point and realized the virtues of a once-slighted Anglican ethos. The growing evangelical affirmation of Anglicanism reflects a series of discoveries along similar lines – namely, that a catholic church order is highly conducive to evangelical fervour. The old-fashioned idea of Anglicanism as a *via media* between "Roman Catholicism" and "Protestantism" needs to be replaced by a creative synthesis of "catholicism" and "evangelicalism" – a development that is happening at parish level, even if Anglican self-awareness and theological reflection has yet to catch up with this welcome development.

The four developments discused in this chapter are all to be dated within the last two or three decades. Their long-term implications are enormous, and cannot be ignored by anyone who is concerned for the future of Anglicanism. The goal-posts have been moved, decisively and irreversibly, in the last few decades. I believe that the outcome of this will be the renewal and regeneration of Western Anglicanism. It certainly needs that kind of renewal, as the considerations to be presented in the following chapter will make clear.

2

A Lost Generation

I was born in 1953, the year in which the English church and nation celebrated the coronation of Elizabeth II. A generation separates that date and the year in which I have found time to write this book. In the view of many, it is a lost generation, that has bequeathed to its successors the task of reconstructing a ruined church throughout the West. The last forty years have been a period of experimental wanderings in the wilderness. However, Israel found and entered its promised land; radical Anglican theology found only a dead end.

I have no memories of Anglicanism during the 1950s. I was growing up in rural Ireland, with no interest in matters of religion. There has, however, been no shortage of studies of the church during this period, nor have those who lived through it been reluctant to pass on their recollections of this age in the history of English Anglicanism. There was no sign of any future decline in the 1950s. The Church of England was in a confident mood. Everything seemed to be going its way. The postwar feeling of optimism persisted. Growth was the watchword of the day – growth in congregational numbers, the number of ordinands, and the income of the church. In his magisterial survey of English Christianity at this juncture, Adrian Hastings captures the mood of confidence and expectation that then enveloped the church, seeing this reflected supremely in the enthronement of Michael Ramsey as archbishop of Canterbury on June 27, 1961.[1] That same year, a radical young Cambridge theologian named Don Cupitt argued vigorously for abandoning belief in Satan. Ambrose Reeves, bishop of Johannesburg and a tireless campaigner against apartheid in South Africa, was appointed General Secretary of the Student Christian Movement in the following year, a development widely regarded as heralding a new Christian commitment to the world.

This mood of optimism persisted into 1962 and early 1963. It is tempting to look for a symbol of this optimism, if only to illustrate how clearly it was to be shattered by the massive cultural upheavals of the 1960s and 1970s. There is no shortage of candidates. Since I have spent a decade of my life preparing men and women for ministry in the Church of England, it is perhaps inevitable that I should select the Paul Report of 1964, which dealt with the future of the ordained ministry, including expectations of the number of ordinands.[2] Paul notes that the number of Anglican clergy in England rose from 18,196 in 1951 to 18,749 in 1961. On the basis of these numbers, he argues that the figure would rise to 21,800 in 1971. To meet this anticipated increase, the number of ordinands in training would rise from 642 in 1963 (the latest figure available to Paul) to 831 in 1971. Nothing of the sort happened. Soon the talk was of closing theological colleges, because of the dramatic downward turn in numbers. The smugness of the early 1960s evaporated as the church realized it was faced with possible long-term decline and decay.

England is not an isolated case in relation to these developments. The same numerical and theological trends can be seen throughout the Western world, with much the same consequences for Anglicanism. During the period 1965–88, the Episcopal Church in the United States lost 28.4 percent of its membership – nearly a million people. This was not the largest decline within the mainline denominations: the Christian Church (Disciples) lost 44 percent of its members, although this figure reflects a major internal schism during the period.[3] The same pattern is clear in Australia, where a peak in mainline church membership was reached at about 1960.[4]

There is no shortage of indicators of this dramatic downturn in the fortunes of mainline Christianity in England at the time. It was not long before the Student Christian Movement found itself drifting loose of its Christian moorings. Attempts were made to have the word "Christian" removed from its title. Critics unkindly suggested that S.C.M. stood for "Scarcely Christian Movement." Don Cupitt extended his radical theological program, to the point at which it became clear that it was not merely Satan, but also God, who could be eliminated from Christianity.[5]

Much liberal writing, especially of the 1960s, appears to have been based on the assumption that the prevailing cultural trends were, in fact, enduring ground swells or permanent changes in Western culture. Adrian Hastings suggests that this period merely witnessed a temporary change of cultural mood, that some were foolish enough to treat as a fixed and lasting change in the condition of humanity:

> In retrospect the dominant theological mood of that time in its hasty, slack rather collective sweep reminds one a little painfully of a flight of lemmings . . . A good deal of the more publicized theological writing in the sixties gives the impression of a sheer surge of feeling that in the modern world God, religion, the transcendent, any reliability in the gospels, anything which had formed part of the old "supernaturalist" system, had suddenly become absurd. There were plenty of fresh insights but too little stringent analysis of the new positions. Everything was to be enthusiastically "demythologized" in a euphoria of secularization which was often fairly soft on scholarly rigour.[6]

The comparison with a "flight of lemmings" is distressingly accurate. Looking back, this precipitate and ill-considered abandoning of any element of the transcendent or supernatural can be seen to have paved the way for the rise of the New Age movement. As Ted Peters (Berkeley) has pointed out, the remarkable growth of New Age in areas hitherto dominated by mainline Christianity can, at least in part, be put down to the efforts of a generation of well-intentioned Protestant writers and preachers who set themselves the task of totally eliminating the supernatural, mystical, and transcendent elements from Christianity in what can now be seen, with the benefit of hindsight, to have been a misguided attempt to make Christianity more relevant or palatable to the modern mind.[7]

Westerners got bored with the resulting religion of platitudes and adopted the New Age instead. People got the idea, thanks to the efforts of yesterday's liberals, that Christianity did not possess any supernatural or transcendent dimensions. Then, yearning for precisely those elements and believing that Christianity lacked them, they turned to the mystical religions of the east, to paganism, and to astrology. Liberalism, which set out to make Christianity more relevant to the modern age, sems to have ended up achieving something like the reverse of its stated intention.

The mood persisted into the 1970s. In 1977, a group of liberal writers published a book entitled *The Myth of God Incarnate*. Although the editor of the work (John Hick) was not an Anglican, most of its contributors were. In many ways, the work illustrates the weaknesses of Anglican liberalism at this stage – such as its willful evasion of the new theological trends coming out of Germany. The work itself is alarmingly chauvinist. In one sense, it represents Anglicanism at its worst – refusing to pay attention to other theological traditions. Although the book purports to 'deal with the central Christological question of the incarnation, not one of the major recent German-language contributions to this discussion was noted, nor its significance assessed. One looks utterly in vain for any recognition of the importance of, for example, Wolfhart Pannenberg's *Jesus – God and Man* (1968), or Jürgen Moltmann's *The Crucified God* (1974). These works were readily available in English at the time' their significancs universally acknowledged, and their writers better known than any of the contributors to the volume. So why this studied evasion of such works, and their implications for the doctrine of the incarnation?

36

Wolfhart Pannenberg has shown himself willing to be open to the contribution of Anglican theologians even if the compliment has yet to be repaid. In a recent critique of the Christological views of John Hick, Pannenberg points out that "Hick's proposal of religious pluralism as an option of authentically Christian theology hinges on the condition of a prior demolition of the traditional doctrine of the incarnation." Hick, Pannenberg notes, assumes that this demolition has already taken place, and chides him for his excessive selectivity – not to mention his lack of familiarity with recent German theology – in drawing such a conclusion.[8] That same criticism could be directed against the remaining contributors. Although prepared to take on board much of the agenda associated with Rudolf Bultmann, for example, there appears to have been no recognition of the sustained criticism to which Bultmann's approach had subsequently been subjected within the German theological tradition.[9]

The reaction to *The Myth* neatly illustrates the dead end into which the prevailing theological trends had led. The book delighted non-Christians, perplexed an increasingly irritated Christian public, and convinced many that the dominant religious liberalism had nothing to offer the church or the world. As Adrian Hastings observes:

> If *The Myth* produced excitement, it was principally the smirking excitement of an agnostic world amused to witness the white flag hoisted so enthusiastically above the long-beleaguered citadel of Christian belief, the stunned excitement of the rank and file of weary defenders on learning that their staff officers had so light-heartedly ratted on them. It was hardly surprising that more than one of the contributors soon after ceased, even in a nominal sense, to be Christian believers, or that Don Cupitt, one of the most forceful and publicity minded of the group, published only two years later his commitment to objective atheism.[10]

There was once a time when atheism was an exciting new possibility – some kind of heroic refusal to allow an oppressive social convention to continue, as the once-fashionable Marxist viewpoint suggested. When retired American bishop William Montgomery Brown argued in 1922, on grounds as muddled as they were Marxist, that it was time to "banish the gods from the skies,"[11] considerable excitement resulted. But by the time of *The Myth*, atheism had become rather humdrum and routine. Its pretensions to adventure and heroism had been severely eroded by the loss of faith within the church itself, of which *The Myth* was merely one of many symptoms. The book, which was widely discounted as a theological curiosity rather than a pioneering landmark, pointed to a lack of confidence and sense of direction within the Church of England at the time. To put it bluntly, Anglicanism began to give the impression that it had not the slightest idea what it was there for, or what it had to say to the world.

These same theological trends can be seen to have emerged within the Episcopal Church in the United States. The most celebrated examples are provided by the writings of James Pike, bishop of California, including his *Time for Christian Candor* (1964), which argued for the jettisoning of the Trinity as "excess baggage," and the more vigorous *If This Be Heresy* (1967), which posed a challenge to traditional Christianity along a wider front. More recently the writings of John Shelby Spong, currently bishop of Newark, New Jersey, seem to tread a similar path, even if just about everyone else seems to have abandoned it as outdated and irrelevant. Spong is a bishop with a genius for self-publicizàtion, evident in the hype surrounding his *Rescuing the Bible from Fundamentalism* (1991).[12] This work would probably have been dismissed as utterly inconsequential were its writer not a bishop (a fact heavily emphasized on its front cover). It is as aggressive in its modernity as it is selective and superficial in its argumentation and intolerant and dismissive of the views of others. For example, at one point, Spong tentatively advances the idea that Paul might have been a homosexual. A few pages later, this notion seems to have become an established result of New Testament scholarship, leading Spong to the conclusion that one of the church's greatest teachers was a "rigidly controlled gay male."[13] The hard historical evidence for this dramatic assertion? Nil. One cannot help wondering if the New Testament is being less than subtly massaged here, to fit the sensitivities of a retrospective liberal conscience.

Much the same thing can be seen in his *Born of a Woman* (1992),[14] in which we learn that Mary, far from being a virgin, was a actually a rape victim. The hard historical evidence for this? Again, nil. Yet Spong apparently expects his readers to take his views on board as the assured findings of New Testament scholarship and reconstruct their vision of the Christian faith and life as a result. One cannot help but feel that the reasoned argumentation we have come to expect of the Anglican tradition has here been replaced by a special pleading and petulant assertion, more characteristic of the fundamentalist groups to which Bishop Spong takes such exception. Spong constructs a fantasy world, in which his own vision of a politically correct culture leads him to impose political and social stereotypes upon the New Testament with a fierce and uncritical dogmatism and a lack of scholarly insight and responsibility that many had assumed were associated only with Jerry Falwell. Many had dared to hope that this kind of thing was not typical of Anglicanism.

Spong chooses to present himself as the moral spearhead of modern scholarship, confronting the church with certain unpalatable yet assured facts that demand that it undergo a radical reorientation. Yet the whole exercise rests upon the flimsiest of foundations. The pseudoscholarly character of Spong's approach has been exposed by Oxford New Testament scholar and Anglican theologian N. T. Wright.[15] Commenting on Spong's attempts to cast himself as a persecuted hero standing for the truth in the midst of a fundamentalist ocean, Wright remarks:

> [Spong] rushes on, constructing imaginary historical worlds and inviting us to base our faith and life upon them. If we refuse this invitation he will, no doubt, hurl his favourite abuse-word at us again. But if everyone who disagrees with Spong's book turns out to be a fundamentalist, then I suppose that all the fundamentalist churches in the world would not be

able to contain the new members who would suddenly arrive on their doorsteps.[16]

What, then, are the merits of the approach that Spong advocates? It has evoked applause from many secular writers, who have welcomed its contribution to their anti-Christian agenda, in much the same way as *The Myth of God Incarnate* won faint praise from a similar audience. Spong also provides a new definition of a fundamentalist (someone who disagrees with Bishop Spong), that has still to win universal assent. But this pugnacious, dismissive, and intolerant work has done nothing to further our understanding of the Gospels, enhance the status of Anglican theology, or contribute to the renewal of Anglicanism. It lacks the generosity of spirit, tolerance, and careful learning and scholarship that have been the hallmarks of Anglican writing through the centuries. No Anglican can afford to allow the good name of Anglican scholarship to be wrecked by this "amazingly caricatured picture of church history," in which "pure fantasy" replaces meticulous and responsible historical inquiry.[17]

Yet Spong is appreciative of at least one fact of major importance. Those who have defended liberal approaches to Christianity, especially during the 1960s and 1970s, often pointed to the apologetic advantages they believe they confer. Liberalism, they argued, represents an attempt to state the Christian faith in terms that will make sense to modern humanity. Traditional Christianity lacked contemporary cultural credibility; culturally accommodated versions of Christianity were thus declared to hold the key to cultural acceptability and numerical growth in the modern period. By the end of the 1980s it was perfectly obvious that that was not the case. Just about the only forms of Christianity that were achieving numerical growth were conservative in orientation. Furthermore, it became clear that liberalism made its case for the cultural accommodation of Christianity on the basis of a false antithesis: either we adapt Christian ideas to modern culture, or we perish. As the Willow Creek experiment in Chicago has made abundantly clear, there are other possibilities, such as the use of culturally acceptable means of presentation of the gospel, while retaining the fundamental ideas of Christianity unchanged.[18]

But Spong does not even suggest that his approach will lead to growth of any kind. Spong himself is quite clear that his ideas will not lead to the renewal of Anglicanism at the numerical level.

> The only churches that grow today are those that do not, in fact, understand the issues, and can therefore traffic in certainty. They represent both the fundamentalistic Protestant groups and the rigidly controlled conservative Catholic traditions. The churches that do attempt to interact with the emerging world are for the most part the liberal Protestant mainline churches that shrink every day in membership and the silent liberal Catholic minority that attracts very few adherents. Both are, almost by definition, fuzzy, imprecise and relatively unappealing. They might claim to be honest, but for the most part they have no real message. They tinker with words, redefine concepts, and retreat slowly behind the rear guard protection of a few pseudoradical thinkers. I have sought to live in this arena. It shrinks daily.[19]

And it is hardly surprising. Any church that "has no real message," or that manages to make the gospel "relatively unappealing," deserves to fail. How can anyone make the "pearl of great price" something that has no attraction for people? Spong has achieved the miracle of turning wine into water, by degrading the gospel into a form of cultural puritanism. The rather smug assumption behind Spong's assertions is that the extent of one's popular appeal is inversely proportional to "understanding the issues." This facile modernism, which dominated academic theological thinking in the 1960s and 1970s, has now widely fallen from favour. The rise of postliberalism is a telling sign of the massive intellectual realignment that is now taking place in North America and beyond.

Bishop Spong recognizes that his views are unpopular, and believes that this is because they are thoroughly up-to-date and intellectually respectable. Sadly, they are just unpopular. They are out of touch with scholarship, the Christian tradition, and the *consensus fidelium.* In fact, for many Spong represents a parody of Anglicanism, that has always taken care to combine intellectual integrity with a deep respect for the Christian tradition and a firm anchoring of theology in the pastoral concerns of the church. Those who wish to renew Anglicanism cannot afford to follow the path trodden by Bishop Spong. It is an utterly fantastic creation, as capricious as its creator, resting upon special pleading, superficial engagement with issues, and a dogmatic imposition of a preconceived agenda upon the New Testament material, which does not even have the merit of popular appeal. Spong runs the risk of making fundamentalism seem intellectually respectable in comparison with Anglicanism. The quality of a church's thinking is not to be judged by how radical or politically correct its conclusions might be, but by the caliber of its scholarship, the judiciousness of its reasoning, and its rootedness in the Christian tradition. In the past, classical Anglicanism has provided a model for such thinking; the time has come to pick up this tradition of excellence and responsibility and make it our own once more.

Curiously, Spong's culturally accommodated response seems to have arisen at a time at which a new cultural shift has emerged, outdating that response even as it was appearing. (Admittedy, these changes have taken place largely in the academic world, and so have yet to filter down to popular writers.) In their light, Spong seems to have shut the stable door after the horse has died. Spong's approach reminds one, to use Hasting's image, of a lemming who, not wishing to be left out of the fun, has joined the party, only to discover that it has fizzled out.

Yet it is ultimately as pointless as it is easy to demonstrate the utter futility of Spong's approach. There are deeper issues at stake here. Anglicanism came to would do well to consider carefully the origins of the cultural shifts to which Spong has belatedly and uncritically responded, asking why they arose and what may be learned from them. The results will be less sensationalist and headline grabbing than some would like; they are, however, likely to lay the foundations for an informed and critical process of reconstruction for Anglicanism in the West.

Understanding Cultural Shifts

Why did these major changes in mood take place in the 1960s and beyond? What happened to bring about this desire for some kind of radical rethinking of Christian theology in the West? We have already spent some time exploring the situation in England and the United States. Let us now turn to the Australian scene, where much the same trends developed over the period in question. These have been subjected to careful study by Australian social psychologist Hugh Mackay. In a recent study entitled *Reinventing Australia* (1993), Mackay sets out his findings, and explores what their implications might be for the future of his country.[20]

Mackay identifies six areas in which settled Australian understandings of society, and individual roles within it, have been shaken to their foundations since the 1960s:

1 Redefinition of gender roles in the wake of the women's movements;
2 Redefinition of the family unit in the light of the rapidly increasing divorce rate;
3 Redefinition of the work ethic on account of the growing impact of unemployment;
4 Loss of egalitarianism through an emerging new rich class, alongside an expanding poor class, created through the rising unemployment rate;
5 Redefining of Australian cultural identity in response to the rise of multiculturalism;
6 Rampant cynicism about the Australian political system.[21]

This has, according to Mackay, led to widespread insecurity about what it means to be "Australian" and an almost tangible sense of anxiety about the future.

Mackay's solution to this dilemma is related to his analysis of what went wrong in the 1960s. The "do your own thing" of the 1960s was easily transposed into the "greed is good" outlook of the 1980s – so familiar in Margaret Thatcher's Britain and Ronald Reagan's America, and memorably lampooned in Tom Wolfe's

Bonfire of Vanities. The "Me Generation," to use Mackay's term (which he may have borrowed from Tom Wolfe's 1976 work *The Purple Decades*), had no interest in the restraints of tradition or the communal dimensions of life. Everything had to center on the needs and demands of the individual. Whether those demands were ethical, financial or religious, the same pattern emerges: I want to do my own thing – and to hell with anything that gets in the way.

> The Me Generation saw themselves not only as radicals but as idealists. They were intent not merely on shaking the foundations of the culture they had inherited from the Forties and Fifties; they were determined to create a new world of their own . . . The Me Generation saw itself as idealistic. but in the end, generally settled for only one ideal: self-fulfilment. Encouraged by the economic and cultural optimism of the 1960s, these Australians embraced a hedonistic self-centeredness which may have sounded and felt to them like idealism, but which lacked the complexity or sensitivity which any value-system was going to need if it was to be an effective resource for coping with the pressures and uncertainties of the Seventies and Eighties.[22]

The cultural values and attitudes of earlier generations were discarded as a matter of principle, rather than as the result of a long and considered process of careful evaluation. Iconoclasm was substituted for argument, as was the individual's perception of things for the communal insights of tradition.

The result is what Mackay tellingly terms a "full-blown mid-life crisis" for the "Me Generation." They are not merely witnessing a rejection of their values by their children, who are increasingly convinced of the merits of a "back to basics" traditionalism; they are also discovering that they themselves no longer believe in those values.

> The Me Generation are beginning to acknowledge that the process of value-shedding through the Sixties and Seventies has left them with a vague sense of emptiness – a feeling that life

44

lacks some of the meaning and the sense of purpose . . .
which they observed in their own much-maligned parents and
grandparents. Facing their own mid-life crisis, the Me
Generation are beginning to have some regrets about . . . their
lack of a coherent framework for dealing with the uncertainties
of life in the last decade of this century.[23]

The theological trends of the 1960s can be seen to fit easily into
this "doing your own thing" style. With the benefit of hindsight,
they can be discerned to be little more than a collective expression
of impatience with tradition, a sort of religious restlessness which
sought self-legitimation partly in the name of alleged "theological
sophistication," but predominantly to achieve cultural acceptability.
Now that party is over, in Australia as everywhere else in the
West. At the religious level, Mackay points to the booming
fundamentalist churches in Australia's suburbs as evidence of the
failure of the trends of the 1960s. The old ideas are making a
comeback. There is a hunger for something that is obviously
missing, and which the Me Generation has realized it cannot
provide.

Mackay has no time for fundamentalism of any shape or size,
whether religious, atheist, or feminist.[24] Yet he points out that
many Australians believe that there is an urgent need to rediscover
traditional values and find some way of incorporating them into
everyday life.[25] This is not the same as a wish to turn back the
clock; rather, it is a desire to maintain continuity with the past, and
regain ideas and values that were uncritically and precipitately
abandoned in the white heat of radical enthusiasm in the 1960s.

The result of all this is clear. The postwar generation seems,
to those who followed on from it, to have squandered opportunities
and lost contact with the gospel itself. The somewhat slight degree
of short-term cultural accommodationism achieved by such writers
hardly seems worth the price paid. Anglicanism, in common with
most mainline churches, has seen its numbers spiral to
threateningly low levels in many parts of the Western world, while
their numbers are increasing dramatically in the developing world,
in which the Enlightenment-inspired pressure for cultural

accommodation has been slight or nonexistent. It remains an open question whether the theological trends that erupted in the West during the 1960s reflected or caused this sense of religious unease and insecurity. That is an issue that can be left to the historians to decide. But what is clear is this: those theological trends are incapable of reversing the membership decline within Anglicanism. They have nothing to offer the modern church.

Then what are younger Anglicans, such as I, to do? We have hardly been set an inspiring example by those older than us. There are indeed Anglican writers who have laid the foundations for renewal and recovery by refusing to go along with the latest cultural trend, such as John Macquarrie and the late Eric L. Mascall. In identifying the need for reconstruction, I am acutely conscious of a lack of role models in the previous generation. Yet African and Asian Anglicanism offers us the vision of an expanding, socially committed church, with a real vision of what the Christian gospel in general, and its Anglican embodiment in particular, could mean for the world. Is it any wonder that many of us are turning to the developing world for role models and an inspirational vision?

There is, then, an urgent and real need for the renewal and reconstruction of Anglicanism in the West. To some observers, it has totally lost its vision, its sense of direction, and any real feeling of purpose; to others, including me, it has merely temporarily mislaid them and can, in principle, recover them. This latter approach is also associated with Stanley Hauerwas and William H. Willimon, who point to the new sense of purpose that the recovery of Christian roots brings:

We are invited to see ourselves and our lives as *part of God's story*. That produces people with a cause . . . Under such a story, life ceases to be the grim, just-one-damn-thing-after-another, sort of existence we have known before. The little things of life – marriage, children, visiting an eighty-year-old nursing home resident, listening to a sermon– are redeemed and given eschatological significance.[26]

So where does the process of reconstruction begin? It seems to me that there is a real urgency to begin this process by addressing the concept of a "middle way" so beloved of Anglican writers of the past. If ever there was a need for a *via media*, allowing us to steer a middle course between two extremes, it is today. This matter is explored in a later chapter. But first, attention is directed to the impact of the Decade of Evangelism, which offers Anglicanism the opportunity to turn its back on a long period of decline or stagnation and to work towards spiritual, theological, and numerical renewal.

3

Evangelism
and
The Renewal of Anglicanism

"The church," wrote Emil Brunner, "lives by mission as a fire lives by burning." Mission is something intrinsic to the identity of the church – not an optional add-on, but something that is part and parcel of the very being of the church. The church exists for many reasons – and one such reason is being the bearer and proclaimer of the good news of Jesus Christ. In the West, this aspect of the task of the church has been neglected, for pragmatic reasons. In a monolithically Christian culture there seemed to be little point or need in proclaiming the gospel. But that situation is changing in the West, and has in any case never applied to Anglicanism in Africa or Asia. The Decade of Evangelism presents us with the opportunity of recollecting – in the dual sense of "remembering" and "picking up again" – this neglected element of the doctrine of the church. Why is the church there? In part, to bring to the world the good news of what God has done, and is doing, though the life, death, and resurrection of Jesus Christ. In the words of the Lambeth report, "The dominant model of the church within the Anglican Communion is a pastoral one. . . . The pressing needs of today's world demand that there be a massive shift to a "mission" orientation throughout the communion."[1] This shift in perspective, with all that it entails, holds the key to the renewal of Anglicanism.

The Mainline Acceptance of Evangelism

There has been a major turnabout in mainline Christian attitudes toward evangelism in the last generation. Let me illustrate this point with reference to events in the United States some forty years ago. In the first quarter of 1954, the evangelist Billy Graham was invited to speak at Union Theological Seminary in New York. By that time Graham had attracted considerable attention.[2] The success of the 1949 Los Angeles Crusade had been widely reported in the secular press, giving Graham a high profile. Union Theological Seminary, a bastion of mainline Protestantism, would hardly be expected to receive him warmly. Graham spoke for forty-five minutes in the seminary chapel, and answered questions afterward for another thirty minutes. When he had finished, he was greeted with one of the longest and most enthusiastic ovations that institution had ever known.[3] It seemed to many that evangelism had suddenly become respectable.

Yet not everyone at Union Theological Seminary was pleased with this development. The noted theologian Reinhold Niebuhr, who had jointed the faculty of Union as professor of Christian ethics in 1927, was distinctly disgruntled about the growing enthusiasm for evangelism. He wrote scathingly of Graham's theological incompetence and naivete.

Billy Graham is a personable, modest and appealing young man who has wedded considerable dramatic and demagogic gifts with a rather obscurantist version of the Christian faith. His message is not completely irrelevant to the broader social issues of the day – but it approaches irrelevance. For what it may be worth, we can be assured that his approach is free of the vulgarities which characterized the message of Billy Sunday, who intrigued the nation about a quarter century ago. We are grateful for this much "progress."[4]

50

Niebuhr's peremptory dismissal of Graham was seen by many as little more than sour grapes on the part of an academic theologian fearful of being marginalized by the new enthusiasm for evangelism. None other than the president of this same Union Theological Seminary, Henry P. van Dusen, weighed in with a response that was probably as devastating as it was unexpected.

> Dr Niebuhr prefers Billy Graham to Billy Sunday. There are many, of whom I am one, who are not ashamed to testify that they would probably have never come within the sound of Dr Niebuhr's voice or the influence of his mind if they had not been *first* touched by the message of the earlier Billy. Quite probably five or ten years hence there may appear in the classrooms and churches of Billy Graham's severest critics not a few who will be glad to give parallel testimony to his role in *starting* them in that direction.[5]

As if that were not enough, it was followed up by a spirited attack on Niebuhr by E. G. Homrighausen, dean of Princeton Theological Seminary. Writing in the leading liberal journal *Christian Century*, Homrighausen, head of the National Council of Churches" Department of Evangelism, accused Niebuhr and his sympathizers of being "hesitant and weak in calling persons to a positive faith." Niebuhr could, he suggested, learn some useful lessons from Billy Graham. Why, he asked, was "Niebuhrian neo-orthodoxy" so hesitant over calling people to conversion?

> I have, frankly, been disappointed in its inability to lead the way in the revival or rebirth or restoration of a relevant Protestantism in the local church. And if men like Graham have arisen, and are being heard by the thousands, it may be that what he is and says in sincerity ought to be said in a better way by the neo-orthodox with all their accumulation of intelligence about the Bible and history and personality in our times.[6]

The point being made was that Niebuhr was parasitic, feeding off the fruits of the work of earlier evangelists without "calling persons to a positive faith" himself.

Anglicanism has been one of the greatest beneficiaries from this new trend toward evangelism. John Stott, the late David Watson, and Michael Green are examples of global evangelists who happen to be Anglicans. The last-mentioned went on to become the first professor of evangelism at Regent College, Vancouver, thus establishing an Anglican in this globally significant position. Furthermore, the impact of Billy Graham on Anglicanism has been considerable. The Harringey crusade of 1954 and the Sydney crusade of 1959 brought new spiritual and numerical strength to Anglicanism in both England and Australia.

The mainstream prejudice against evangelism is gradually fading into history. Evangelism is increasingly seen as a normal part of the life of the church. And with this development comes a major stimulus to the renewal of Anglicanism – discovering what it is about the Christian faith that makes it attractive to outsiders in the first place.

Evangelism and Rediscovering the Good News

The Christian gospel is good news – something that has the power to transform the lives of women and men and gladden their hearts. One of the most significant results of the Decade of Evangelism has been to force ordinary Christians to ask what it is about the Christian faith that makes it attractive to them and to others. The very suggestion that people might wish to *become* Christians is quite unsettling for many in Western culture, largely because of the dominance of purely pastoral and social models of the church. Many Western Christians react with surprise to the suggestion that their non-Christian colleagues and family members might one day choose to become Christians.

Many secular writers have responded with a certain degree of tetchiness to the idea of a concentration upon the task of evangelism. Some have reached for the nearest cliché to hand and written of "Christian imperialism"; others have suggested that the churches have become obsessed with marketing their product, presenting evangelism as some kind of religious public relations industry. Both these comments are deeply revealing of the failure of an increasingly secular society to understand the fundamental motivation for evangelism. For there is something intrinsically attractive about the Christian faith and, supremely, about the person of Jesus Christ. It is like a "pearl of great price," something that is recognized to be worth seeking and possessing, and whose possession overshadows everything else. The fundamental motivation for evangelism is that of generosity – the basic human concern to share the good things of life with those whom we love. It does not reflect a desire to sell or dominate; it arises from love and compassion on the part of those who have found something wonderful and want others to share in its joy. It is, as the old adage has it, like one beggar telling another where to find bread.

Some older Anglicans in the West have reacted negatively to this new emphasis, seeing it as a partisan development, reflecting the special concerns of the evangelical wing of the church. Yet evangelism is not the prerogative or privilege of one section of the church; it is something to which the church, as a whole, is called, and from which the whole church will benefit. Pope John Paul II, not usually thought of as an evangelical, has stressed the importance of evangelism for the church as it seeks to make the good news of Jesus Christ known to the world. In his encyclical letter *Redemptoris Missio*, Pope John Paul II stressed that "proclamation is the permanent priority of mission. The Church cannot elude Christ's explicit mandate, nor deprive men and women of the "Good News" about their being loved and saved by God."[7] It is, in fact, the *refusal* to accept the evangelistic challenge of the gospel that is partisan in spirit. If evangelism has become the exclusive preserve of one section of the church, that is to be seen as the direct consequence of its neglect elsewhere. The Decade offers the church the opportunity to reclaim this responsibility.

The Decade of Evangelism has alerted many ordinary believers to the impact that Christianity can have upon those who discover it for the first time. Probably through excessive familiarity, many Western Anglicans have become dulled to the wonder of the Christian story. The Decade has reminded us that, although that story may be all too familiar to us, there are others who have yet to hear it. Many Anglicans are only now discovering that something that they had taken for granted can have a dramatic impact on those outside the church, often being taken aback at the delight and joy with which their friends respond to the Christian faith.

Yet evangelism does not affect merely those to whom the good news is proclaimed. As the 1988 Lambeth Conference noted, "both evangelists and the evangelized are transformed by a fresh apprehension of the Good News."[8] The Decade of Evangelism provides a window of opportunity for those who are already Christians, by providing them with an opportunity to appreciate the Christian faith. For Lambeth challenges us to discover the full depths of our own faith. It invites us to open the treasure chest of the Christian tradition, to which Anglicanism has made a distinctive and valued contribution, and appreciate the wonder and sheer *attraction* of the Christian gospel. Far too many Christians, including Anglicans, have at best only a superficial appreciation and understanding of their faith. The call to evangelize is a call to ask ourselves the following question: What is it about the gospel that is "good news"? What is there about Christianity that should make other people want to come to faith? To ask such questions is potentially to open the door to new and enhanced appreciation of our own faith. Sadly, overfamiliarity has dulled our appreciation for the Christian faith.

A colleague of mine, who had spent many years working in Oxford, decided to emigrate and settle in another part of the world. After a few years, however, he returned to Oxford. Puzzled, I asked him why. He looked sheepish. "I never really appreciated how beautiful a place Oxford was till I left it. I just took it for granted. I imagined that other places had to be better. But they weren't. So I came home." Many Anglicans are like that. cThey just take Christianity for granted. They do not appreciate how attractive it could be for outsiders. They've got used to it, and fail to see why anyone outside the church could be deeply attracted by it. The Decade provides a long-overdue stimulus to Western Anglicanism to reawaken its interest in the Christian gospel itself.

Evangelism and the Renewal of Faith

Faith comes in two styles. In the first place, faith may be understood as the body of Christian beliefs, the "faith which is believed *(fides quae creditur)*." Evangelism is an invitation to all Anglicans to master their own faith, to be "prepared to give an answer to everyone who asks you to give the reason for the hope that you have" (1 Peter 3:15).

One of the most exciting consequences of the new emphasis on evangelism within the Anglican churches is that it has encouraged Christians to find out more about their faith. It is much easier to explain something if you have thought about it yourself. A good understanding of Christianity can bring a new quality and depth to evangelism, whether this takes the form of major meetings or simply everyday discussions with your friends over coffee. But there is a major fringe benefit here. I gave a lecture recently, on "Making Sense of the Cross" to a group drawn from several churches in Geneva, Switzerland. I pointed out how some of the ideas I was exploring would enable members of the audience to explain Christianity far more effectively to their friends. Someone came up to me afterwards. "I don't know whether what you told us will help me evangelize folks," he said, "but it sure helped me to see things clearer!"

One of the results of taking trouble to get to know more about Christianity is that our own faith is enriched and deepened. Evangelism does not just bring people to faith – it deepens the faith of those who already believe. It gives a new motivation and quality to Christian education, that can otherwise seem curiously unfocused and devoid of purpose. The new emphasis upon evangelism has changed all this. It has opened the door to the renewal of Anglicanism at the individual level, by providing a motivating focus for delving into the richness of our past in order to enrich the present and enable the church in its role. As Lambeth pointed out, "There are whole armies of lay people in our churches to be revitalized."[9] Evangelism provides the occasion and motivation for this much needed and overdue revitalization.

But there is also faith in the sense of "the faith which believes (*fides qua creditur*)." Defining this kind of faith is notoriously difficult. Richard Hooker offered a measured and thoughtful definition of faith when he wrote of it as being "the only hand that putteth on Christ."[10] Faith is here understood as a personal commitment, an inward appropriation, not so much of the basic elements of Christian faith, but of the greater reality to which those bear witness – namely, Christ himself. At the risk of appearing to be theologically unsophisticated, faith in this sense of the term is basically *trust*. Lambeth issued this challenge: "In every diocese of our Communion, we are called urgently – today – to renewed faith in him who sends us to proclaim the message of God's love."[11] The call to evangelize is a call to renew our personal and corporate faith in God – to develop a sense of expectation and anticipation of what God can do in and through us.

One of the finest discussions of this aspect of faith is offered by A. C. A. Hall, a former bishop of Vermont. In his *Doctrine of the Church* (1909), Hall spoke of faith in terms that develop Hooker's notion in a direction that would command widespread assent today.

> Christian faith means more than mere intellectual assent. It stands for the acceptance by the whole man, in mind and heart and will, of the divine word, so that the man shall be molded by the truth revealed. Further still, faith is specially used of a relation and attitude towards a *person*. In this sense, it means not only belief that such a one exists, and belief that what he states is true, but also the trustful surrender of ourselves to the person in whom we believe . . . It is to faith of this kind directed toward God and our Lord Jesus Christ that the great promises in the New Testament are made.[12]

Evangelism allows this second aspect of the Christian understanding of faith to be appreciated to its full, and encourages us to *trust* more in the God who has called us to follow him.

Evangelism thus leads directly to renewal, at both the personal and corporate levels. It offers us an opportunity to discover more about the Christian gospel and to realize its potential for humanity. It also invites us to deepen our personal commitment to the Christian faith. Yet it does more than this; it also draws attention to the distinctive character of Anglicanism, that has equipped it to benefit fully from its overdue rediscovery of evangelism. In particular, the Anglican confluence of evangelicalism and catholicism within the same church body is proving to be of strategic importance as it turns to adopt a posture of mission in the years ahead. This point is explored in the following discussion.

Evangelism and the Dynamics of Anglicanism

Of particular importance within Anglicanism has been the recent establishment of the *Springboard* initiative by the Archbishops of Canterbury and York. This initiative gives a much needed theological and pastoral direction to the Decade of Evangelism. *Springboard* is headed up by Michael Green and Bishop Michael Marshall, two senior figures within English Anglicanism, yet with extensive experience of the North American situation as well.

As the *Springboard* initiative has developed, increasing attention has come to focus on a threefold movement within an overall evangelistic strategy: *apologetics*, leading into *evangelism*, leading into *spirituality*. Apologetics ensures that Christianity is regarded as a credible option in society; evangelism provides an opportunity for individuals to make a personal response to the gospel; spirituality provides new believers with the resources they need to keep going – and to keep growing – in the Christian life. Each of these three activities happens to have a long association with a particular wing of the Anglican church.

The Mainline Contribution: Apologetics

One of the greatest strengths of Anglicanism in the past has been its commitment to apologetics – the deliberate and principled attempt to make Christianity credible and relevant to the modern world. Alan Richardson's *Christian Apologetics* (1947) represents a classical Anglican approach to the subject, that addresses the critical issues being raised in the postwar period.[13] If any section of Anglicanism has taken this task with particular seriousness in the past, it has been its mainline or central wing (I avoid using the term "liberal" on account of its negative present-day overtones.) Leading writers belonging to this section of the church – such as John Habgood in England and Norman Pittenger in the United States – have placed considerable emphasis on the need for the church to maintain its public intelligibility and credibility. In the past, lay Anglicans, including Dorothy L. Sayers and C. S. Lewis, have made a major contribution to this central task of the church.[14] More recently, Professor John Polkinghorne, an Anglican priest who was formerly professor of mathematical physics at the University of Cambridge, has produced a series of highly acclaimed works of major apologetic importance, focusing on the relation of Christianity and the natural sciences,[15] as has Hugh Montefiore, a former bishop of Birmingham, England.[16]

There is a continuing need to take rational trouble to relate Christianity to prevailing cultural trends and to our developing understanding of reality as a whole. This, it must be stressed, does not mean uncritically endorsing or capitulating to these trends, as if Christianity were a bull being led meekly by a ring through its nose in whatever direction culture wanted to take it. The experience of the German churches under Hitler has ruled out that option. Rather, it means seeking to make Christianity credible in terms of whatever values or ideas contemporary culture, in all its diversity, recognizes as having authority or weight. Those sections of Anglicanism that take contemporary culture most seriously are potentially best placed to make this contribution to the evangelistic tasks of the church. They have a real and valued role to play and must be given every encouragement to do so.

The Evangelical Emphasis: Evangelism
Evangelicalism is without question the powerhouse of evangelistic endeavor within the modern Christian church, in England and

elsewhere. Time and time again, people attribute their discovery of the vitality and excitement of the gospel to the witness of evangelicalism. Richard Holloway, bishop of Edinburgh and primus of the Scottish Episcopal Church, is but one of many recent writers outside evangelicalism to pay tribute to its commitment and success in evangelization.[17] It is here that evangelicalism finds a distinctive and important role within Anglicanism.

The presence of an active evangelical element within Anglicanism is of major importance to the growth of that church, especially in the West. Young people who come to faith as students tend to be drawn into churches in which they feel there is a concern for mission and outreach. The presence of evangelicalism as a significant and valued element in Anglicanism will attract into the mainstream of Anglicanism committed and highly motivated young men and women, often with an enthusiasm and passion for ministry, who might otherwise find their way into other churches. While one would rejoice at the enrichment thus brought to those churches, one could only mourn the resulting impoverishment of Anglicanism. An active commitment to evangelism will ensure that Anglicanism is enriched in this way.

The Catholic Contribution: Spirituality

Having brought people to faith, the church must ensure that they are provided with the resources they need to grow in faith. There is a real need to take the pressures and realities of Christian living in the modern period seriously enough to devise spiritual strategies to allow new and struggling Christians to cope with them. Evangelism makes Christians; spirituality keeps them.

A case study from the United States illustrates the importance of this point. It is generally recognized that the only churches that are growing in the United States are evangelical in orientation; indeed, for many secular observers, "evangelical" has become synonymous with "active and growing." But some – admittedly, very few – churches of a much more liberal orientation are also expanding. An example is All Saints Episcopal Church, Pasadena,[18] that has received widespread media attention because it bucks the trend. It is one of the very few growing liberal congregations within the mainline denominations in the United States. Its liberalism is not in doubt; it is strongly pro-choice in its attitude toward abortion, and it made international headlines in November 1990 when its rector announced that he would begin performing blessings in church of "same-sex" couples.

Why is this church growing, when it is not evangelical? Just about every other church with such liberal social commitments is losing members in droves. Because the phenomenon is so unusual, it has been studied with particular care. Donald E. Miller, professor of religion at the University of Southern California's school of religion, puts his finger on the point at issue: although the church is liberal in its politics, "it is also deeply conservative in its recognition of the importance of worship, pastoral care, and personal spiritual disciplines."[19] Attention to the personal spiritual needs and concerns of its individual members have been the key in this situation. People need help with prayer, devotion and personal discipline. All Saints provides this, where others have not.

The catholic wing of the Anglican churches has a long tradition of spiritual direction, that takes full account of the need for individual care and nurture in this respect.[20] Richard Holloway is an example of a writer within this tradition who has made a distinguished and valued contribution in this field, that has been well-received throughout the spectrum of Anglican opinion.[21] It is here that this tradition can make a distinctive and valued contribution to the needs of the Decade of Evangelism.

A concern for spirituality, however, need not be confined to the catholic wing of Anglicanism, any more than evangelism need be confined to its evangelical wing. All three components could, and arguably should, be the exclusive prerogative of none. Yet my concern has been to point out how each of the three wings of Anglicanism can draw upon emphases that, as a matter of historical fact, have been characteristic of their self-understandings. By being themselves, they can aid the renewal of Anglicanism. Evangelism provides a focus upon which the three distinctive elements of Anglicanism can find a natural and organic convergence.

Evangelism and Christian Unity

The new emphasis on evangelism is also a vital impulse towards greater Christian cooperation and a genuine motivating factor toward achieving Christian unity. Lambeth 1988 acknowledged the transparently obvious fact that ecumenism, once the major theme of Christian gatherings, has become boring and of little relevance to most ordinary Christians. It has become seen as the preoccupation of church bureacracies and committees and perceived as being out of touch with grass-roots sentiments.

> Too often preoccupation with negotiations to restore the institutional union of denominations, separated in the distant past, has failed to capture the imagination and fire the enthusiasm of Anglicans. We need to ask what the church is for; and only if its purpose demands closer unity will we be moved actively to work for such unity.[22]

Most ordinary Christians have little interest in institutional unity. They are, however, interested in drawing closer to other Christians and working alongside them in shared tasks. Michael Green, one of the co-ordinators of the *Springboard* initiative for the Decade of Evangelism, has noted how a common concern for evangelism and mission brings churches of all denominations, from Baptists to Roman Catholics, together in a common concern to preach the Christian gospel. Denominational differences are seen as being transcended by this common task and concern. My own work worldwide, directed toward the enabling and equipping of Christians for mission and ministry, is conducted on virtually totally transdenominational lines. Giving priority or even attention to denominational distinctions is seen to detract and distract from the common shared tasks of all Christians.

It has often been said, but needs to be said once more, that what Christians have in common is far more important than what divides them. Evangelism has the glorious and liberating effect of bringing into high relief what all Christian share – "the exuberance of the joy we have experienced in being healed, restored, forgiven and freed from bondage," as Lambeth puts it.[23] The encyclical *Redemptoris Missio* speaks movingly of the full riches of the gospel, in terms that all Christians can easily accept and affirm:

> The subject of proclamation is Christ who was crucified, died and is risen: through him is accomplished our full and authentic liberation from evil, sin and death; through him God bestows "new life" that is divine and eternal. This is the "Good News" which changes humanity and their history and which all peoples have a right to hear.[24]

Such an affirmation carries universal appeal and authority to Christians, providing a focused and motivating issue on which they can unite in the shared task of evangelization. Although ecumenical committees have achieved much, they have by and large failed to inspire ordinary Christians. The call to share the common task and commission of evangelization affects ordinary people in ways that distant committees, so often seen to be dominated by academics and church bureaucrats, have failed to do.

This has important implications for the often rehearsed discussion concerning "fundamental articles of faith" or "fundamentals of faith."[25] It is not so much "articles of faith" that Christians have in common, but the redeeming presence of the risen Jesus Christ. *Ubi Christus, ibi ecclesia.* That presence may be conceptualized in various manners, reflecting different local idioms and ways of thinking. Nevertheless, such theologizing is secondary to the Christian experience of Christ and appreciation of his benefits – an experience and appreciation that provide a fundamental impetus for evangelism. Such considerations may not resolve the debate over fundamentals of faith; they do, however, place it in its proper context, by reminding us that the primacy *fundamentum* of faith is Jesus Christ, who is and will always remain prior to attempts to explain him.[26] Evangelism reminds us that this *fundamentum* is no abstract doctrine, no antiquated formula, but a living presence – a presence that lies at the center of Christian proclamation and adoration.

In 1976, the Anglican Consultative Council met in Trinidad and reported on its reflections. Among the issues it explored was how to foster visible unity between the churches. One of the most important *aperçus* of that meeting has passed largely unnoticed: "It has been hitherto assumed that organic union is to be sought for the sake of mission. Our experience seems to be showing that joint action for mission leads to the deepening of commitment to visible unity."[27] Further hints of this realization may be discerned in the 1988 Lambeth Conference, which drew attention to the increasingly obvious fact that "cooperation in faith and service . . . encourages growing agreement in faith."[28] Evangelism provides a natural point of convergence towards unity. Attempts to foster unity for its own sake have proved largely fruitless and have often foundered on the lack of a motivating force to sustain them. The identification of a common task, transcending denominational demarcations, seems far more likely to bring the churches closer together than the decisions of distant committees.

Let us return to the words of Lambeth 1988: "The pressing needs of today's world demand that there be a massive shift to a "mission" orientation throughout the communion."[29] As I suggested earlier, this shift in perspective, with all that it entails, holds the key to the renewal of Anglicanism. A survey of the teaching programs of the theological colleges of the Church of England during the period 1987–92 uncovered a trend of major significance in this respect: "Programmes of theological education are giving increasing emphasis to the *mission* of the church as God's mission in the world and are less dominated by concern with ministry in terms of maintenance and pastoral care."[30]

This development is to be welcomed, not least because it points to a long overdue coming to terms with the reality of the situation confronting world Anglicanism and a reappraisal of the priorities of a church that, historically, has concentrated on and invested in maintenance rather than mission. The same report also noted "an increasing emphasis on training that can equip ordinands to *communicate* their knowledge and understanding to others. This has in view the preparation of ordinands to participate in mission and evangelism."

These are encouraging trends, that indicate that even in England, where a somewhat staid version of Anglicanism prevails, that has until recently been dominated by a pastoral care model of ministry, new priorities are beginning to emerge – priorities that lay the foundations for the renewal of Anglicanism at every level. In April 1994, the Church of England's Advisory Board of Ministry and Board of Mission, mindful of Lambeth's new emphasis on evangelism, have convened a major consultation entitled "Making Christ Known: Mission and Evangelism in Ministerial Education and Training," concerned to assist ordinands to explain and commend the Christian faith. It is clear that the ground is being laid for major positive and progressive development in this vital area.

Yet this new emphasis on evangelism, on the part of individuals and churches, also points ahead to another and perhaps an even greater, hope – the renewal of Anglican theology. In the words of the great German theologian Martin Kähler: "Mission is the mother of theology." Mission indeed holds before us the promise of theological regeneration, by providing a framework of Christian confidence and purpose, that allows theology to emerge as a natural and valued option for the church, instead of being seen simply as the pastime of academics.

As noted earlier, theology is the intellectual self-expression of a community that feels good about itself and wants to express its reason for existence to the world around it. As Anglicanism regains its confidence after the wasted years of the last few decades, it can expect a theological renaissance to get under way. The recovery of a sense of purpose and poise within Anglicanism will inevitably lead to a growing concern to articulate its sense of purpose and identity at a theological level. The following chapters of this book consider aspects of this major theme of the renewal of Anglican theology.

4

The Renewal of Anglican Theology
Addressing Experience

As is often pointed out, the term Anglican theology is somewhat problematical.[1] In the first place, there is a widespread perception that Anglicanism does not possess a distinctive set of doctrines. Traditional Anglican apologetic has placed considerable emphasis upon Anglicanism's commitment to the common teachings of the Christian church and has studiedly avoided the suggestion that there are distinctively Anglican doctrines. "Anglican theology" is often glossed simply as "theology originating from Anglican writers." Furthermore, the suggestion that there are such distinctive doctrines, or – even more significantly – that there is a distinctively Anglican theological method often rests upon a depressingly vague familiarity with the theological traditions of the rest of Christendom, not to mention a lack of graciousness toward other theological traditions within Christianity. Non-Anglicans, especially within the Lutheran and Reformed traditions, are often shocked by what they (mistakenly, one hopes) perceive as the calculated arrogance of Anglicans in laying claim to a common heritage of Christianity and declaring that it is somehow uniquely and normatively "Anglican."

One of the first steps towards the theological renewal of Anglicanism must be the re-examination of our cherished claims to distinctiveness, to ensure that we are not simply perpetuating unjustifiable misjudgments concerning our past heritage. This process may well provide to be painful; it is, however, essential. Anglicanism cannot allow itself to be grounded upon a mythology concerning its own distinctiveness, nor upon caricatures of the positions of others.

Being Realistic about Anglican Theology

There is a liturgy that Anglicans are prone to recite and seem to be reciting increasingly of late.[2] It goes like this.

President:

The *Protestant churches* have erred grievously, in that they attribute authority to Scripture alone. The *Church of Rome* hath also erred grievously, because it attributeth authority only to Tradition, as have the *Rationalists*, who ascribe authority only to Reason. But the *Anglican church* hath got it right, because it disperseth authority among Scripture, Tradition and Reason.

People:

A threefold cord will not be quickly broken.

(There is, however, a rumor that in the process of liturgical revision, this response may be replaced with *A three-legged stool won't fall over all that easily*.) Like all the best liturgical formulations, its origins are lost in the mists of history. However, as Cyprian of Carthage reminded his readers in the third century, an ancient tradition can just be an old mistake.

In the first place, the position outlined in the foregoing exchange is an absurdity. To argue that Protestant theologians base their theology on "Scripture alone" betrays an alarming lack of familiarity with the theology of the sixteenth-century Reformation – a deficiency that my German Lutheran friends in particular take especial delight in pointing out. For example, Luther's theology –

which he himself designated as "the Bible and Augustine" –
represents a creative intermingling of Scripture and tradition, in
which Scripture is read and interpreted within a believing
community of faith, aware of its continuity with an earlier
tradition.[3] Luther's close colleague at Wittenberg, Philip
Melanchthon, saw the Lutheran Reformation as a considered
attempt to reform and renew the catholic tradition, which he
regarded as having departed from the *primum et verum* of apostolic
times. Indeed, Melanchthon saw the Reformation as the sixteenth-
century equivalent of earlier reformations within the church.[4]
Equally, it is absurd to suggest that writers such as Luther
dispensed with "reason" because of their emphasis on Scripture.
Luther mistrusts reason at points, especially on account of the
"commonsense" idea that justification must take place on the basis
of human achievement. A theology founded exclusively upon
reason would, he argues, lead to a doctrine of justification by
works, thereby fatally compromising the gospel of grace. Despite
these anxieties, however, Luther insists that reason has a
significant role to play in theology. *Homini ratio et sermo data
sunt, quorum officium est veritatem dicere.*[5] That same position is
developed in the Reformed tradition, with writers such as
Theodore Beza placing considerable emphasis upon reason as a
theological resource, culminating in the development of a strongly
rational apologetics in seventeenth-century Calvinism.[6]

Similarly, it is simply untenable to suggest that Roman Catholic
theology makes its appeal solely, or supremely, to tradition. The
case of Thomas Aquinas should surely indicate the absurdity of this
stereotype. After all, Aquinas was heavily criticized by Luther for
making so much use of *reason* – not tradition! – in his theology.[7]
Aquinas places enormous emphasis on Scripture, insisting that
theology is, at heart, taking rational trouble over the mystery of
revelation, mediated through Scripture.[8] Again, the great medieval
theologian John Duns Scotus, in many ways a rival to Aquinas,
affirmed that "theology does not concern anything except what is
contained in Scripture and what may be inferred from this."[9]
Recent studies on late medieval thought have stressed the primacy

of Scripture in the theology of the period.[10] So where does this idea that Roman Catholicism appeals only to tradition come from? Sadly, the answer appears to be depressingly mundane: from ill-informed Anglican apologists and popularists. The simple truth of the matter is that all Christian theology has appealed to Scripture, tradition, and reason (generally in that order); the debate has centered on the relationship between the three. An appeal to these three sources is, it must be stressed, most emphatically not a *distinguishing* characteristic of Anglicanism.

In any case, many more recent Anglican writers have felt the need to supplement these three with additional sources, of which experience is particularly important. (The term Wesley Quadrilateral is used in some North American Methodist circles to refer to this grouping of four resources.) The experiential deficit of classical Anglican thought is well-known and was no small contributing cause to the rise of Methodism and "experimental religion" in the eighteenth century. Today, the charismatic movements offer an experience related theology that contrasts sharply with the somewhat cerebral character of much classical Anglican theology, including that of Hooker. Perhaps we have something to learn here from more experientially orientated approaches. This does not mean adopting the strategy of grounding theology totally in the realm of human experience, as advocated by writers such as David Tracy and so severely undermined recently by George Lindbeck.[11] Rather, it means that unless theology is seen to address, interpret and transform human experience, it will be seen as an irrelevance to life.

Addressing Experience

My first major encounter with the classical Anglican tradition dates from the period 1978–80, when I devoured the writings of its apologists as part of my research into the development of the Christian doctrine of justification.[12] As I read and annotated Hooker andrewes and a host of other writers, I found myself delighted, perhaps even fascinated, by their theological perception and confidence. Their exploration of the relation between

Scripture, tradition and reason impressed me as being among the finest I had encountered from that period in Christian history. I also, however, had the sense that something indefinable was wrong somewhere. Somehow, Anglicanism seemed to be – well, terribly *dull*. It evoked for me an image of book-lined studies, quill pens, layers of accumulated dust, and, somewhere amidst its mass of books and papers, the bespectacled denizen of this paper-strewn empire – the theologian. Here, at least to me, seemed to be one who dealt supremely with books and ideas, a bookish person writing for other bookish people. There was no engagement with the human imagination, emotions, or feelings.

Precisely that same difficulty emerged within German Lutheranism during the seventeenth century. Lutheranism had come to locate the touchstone of Christian authenticity in doctrinal orthodoxy, in the sense of conformity to creedal or confessional statements. The resulting theological systems had impeccable theological credentials, but were hopelessly out of touch with the experiential world of ordinary Christians. The rise of Pietism was a direct response to the emotional aridity and sterility of Lutheranism at this time. Pietism's strongly experiential concept of a "living faith" contrasted with the rather boring contemporary Lutheran notion of faith as assent to revealed truth. (This emphasis on "feeling (*das Gefühl*)" emerges in a different form in the writings of F. D. E. Schleiermacher, who famously regarded himself as a "Pietist of a higher order.")

The rise of Methodism in England during the eighteenth century confirmed this experiential deficit of classic Anglicanism. John Wesley propounded an experiential theology (an "experimental religion," as he called it, using the distinctive language of this older age) that was able to link up with the world of working men and women. Perhaps they did not or could not read; but they had feelings, which Wesley was able to address and engage. The rise of Wesleyanism suggests that classical Anglicanism has severe limitations. Theology must engage with experience, if it is to ensure its relevance to a mass public. But how? And what is this "experience" that needs to be addressed?

69

Experience is an imprecise term. The origins of the English word are relatively well understood: it derives from the Latin term *experientia*, that could be interpreted as "that which arises out of traveling through life (*ex-perientia*)." In this broad sense, it means "an accumulated body of knowledge, arising through first-hand encounter with life." When one speaks of "an experienced teacher" or "an experienced doctor," the implication is that the teacher or doctor has learned his or her craft through first hand application.

Yet the term *experience* has developed an acquired meaning, that particularly concerns us here. It has come to refer to the inner life of individuals, in which those individuals become aware of their own subjective feelings and emotions.[13] It relates to the inward and subjective world of experience, as opposed to the outward world of everyday life. A series of writings, including William James's celebrated study *The Varieties of Religious Experience* (1902), have stressed the importance of the subjective aspects of religion in general and Christianity in particular. Christianity is not simply about ideas; it is about the interpretation and transformation of the inner life of the individual. This concern with human experience is particularly associated with the movement generally known as existentialism, that has sought to restore an awareness of the importance of the inner life of individuals to both theology and philosophy.[14]

Two main approaches may be discerned within Christian theology to the question of the relation of experience to theology:

1. Experience provides a foundational resource for Christian theology.

2. Christian theology provides a framework by which human experience may be interpreted.

The first approach has been of major importance within recent liberal theological approaches; the second has a long history of association with mainline Christianity from Augustine onward and is explored later in this chapter. We begin, however, by

70

considering the first position.

Experience as the Foundation of Theology

The idea that human religious experience can act as a foundational resource for Christian theology has obvious attraction. It suggests that Christian theology is concerned with human experience – something that is common to all humanity, rather than the exclusive preserve of a small group. To those who are embarrassed by the "scandal of particularity," the approach has many merits. It suggests that all the world religions are basically human responses to the same religious experience, often referred to as "a core experience of the transcendent." Christian theology is thus the Christian attempt, as Buddhist thought represents another legitimate and valid attempt, to reflect on this common human experience, in the knowledge that the same experience underlies all other world religions. In much the same way, the Bible may be read as part of the history of human experience of the transcendent – not the only history, nor even a normative history, but simply one component part of the great religious heritage of humanity.

This approach also has considerable attraction for Christian apologetics, as the writings of many recent American theologians, especially Paul Tillich and David Tracy, make clear. In that humans share a common experience, whether they choose to regard it as "religious" or not, Christian theology can address this common experience. The problem of agreeing on a common starting point is thus avoided; the starting point is already provided, in human experience. Apologetics can demonstrate that the Christian gospel makes sense of common human experience. This approach is probably seen at its best in Paul Tillich's sermons in *The Courage to Be*, which attracted considerable attention after their publication in 1952. It seemed to many observers that Tillich had succeeded in correlating the Christian proclamation with common human experience.[15]

Yet there are difficulties here. The most obvious is that there is actually very little empirical evidence for a "common core experience" throughout human history and culture. The idea is easily postulated and virtually impossible to verify. This approach has found its most mature and sophisticated expression in the "Experiential-Expressive Theory of Doctrine," to use a term employed by the distinguished Yale theologian George Lindbeck. In his volume *The Nature of Doctrine* (1984), Lindbeck provides an important analysis of the nature of Christian doctrine.[16] One of the many merits of this book is the debate that it has initiated over this unjustly neglected aspect of Christian theology, that has assumed new importance recently because of the impact of the ecumenical movement.

Lindbeck suggests that theories of doctrine may be divided into three general types. The cognitive-propositionalist approach lays stress upon the cognitive aspects of religion, emphasizing the manner in which doctrines function as truth claims or informative propositions. The experiential-expressive approach interprets doctrines as non-cognitive symbols of inner human feelings or attitudes. A third possibilty, that Lindbeck himself favours, is the cultural-linguistic approach to religion. Lindbeck associates this model with a "rule" or "regulative" theory of doctrine. It is Lindbeck's criticism of the second such theory that is of particular interest to us at this point.

The "experiential-expressive" theory, according to Lindbeck, sees religions, including Christianity, as public, culturally conditioned manifestations and affirmations of prelinguistic forms of consciousness, attitudes and feelings. In other words, there is some universal "religious experience," which Christian theology (in common with other religions) attempts to express in words. The experience comes first; the theology comes in later. As Lindbeck argues, the attraction of this approach to doctrine is grounded in a number of features of late twentieth-century Western thought. For example, the contemporary preoccupation with interreligious dialogue is made a lot easier if one assumes that the various world religions are just different ways of expressing a common core experience, such as an "isolable core of encounter" or an "unmediated awareness of the transcendent."

The obvious problem with this theory is its resistance to

verification. The idea of "experience" is so vague that it dies the "death of a thousand qualifications," to use a phrase popularized some time ago by philosopher of religion Anthony Flew. As Lindbeck points out, "religious experience" is a hopelessly vague idea. "It is difficult or impossible to specify its distinctive features and yet unless this is done, the assertion of commonality becomes logically and empirically vacuous." The assertion that "the various religions are diverse symbolizations of one and the same core experience of the Ultimate" is something that cannot be proved or disproved. It is actually a dogma, in the worst sense of the word. How would anyone go about locating and describing the "core experience" concerned, given that it is of such crucial importance? As Lindbeck rightly points out, this would appear to suggest that there is "at least the logical possibility that a Buddhist and a Christian might have basically the same faith, although expressed very differently." The theory can be credible only if it is possible to isolate a common core experience from religious language and behavior and demonstrate that the latter two are articulations of or responses to the former.

Further difficulties with this approach have emerged in recent years. Feminists have expressed outrage that such vague appeals to "commonality" should overlook the issue of *women's* experience. Liberation theologians have dismissed this idea with something approaching contempt: how can anyone seriously suggest that the experience of middle-class American theologians is in any way comparable to the experience of the poor and oppressed in Latin America? A person's social context, to give one example studiously ignored by the Kantian tradition, has a major impact on how experience is interpreted. Similar protests have been made by others, with gender, race, class, language, tradition and culture all being added to the immensely complex debate, that has rendered talk of a "common human experience" utterly vacuous. With such radical questioning of its foundations, it is little surprise that superstructure of a theology grounded solely on a "common human experience" has come cascading to the ground in the last decade.

The liberal appeal to pure uninterpreted global experience is widely regarded as discredited, partly because of the considerations noted by George Lindbeck and others, and partly on account of a new awareness of the implications of the philosophy of Ludwig Wittgenstein. As Stanley Hauerwas remarked, "Wittgenstein ended forever any attempt on my part to try to anchor theology in some general account of human experience."[17] Experience is always "experience *of something*"; there is always an element of interpretation in the act of experiencing. As Edmund Husserl pointed out, this interpretative element may be modifed as the process of interpretation proceeds – yet it is always there, even at its earliest stages.[18] There is simply no such thing as "uninterpreted common human experience." It is a fiction, as imaginary as Robinson Crusoe's desert island.

Yet this widespead disenchantment with experience as a theological resource must not allow us to reject a significant experiential component in theological reflection. Furthermore, as I have argued elsewhere, experience is a vital "point of contact" for Christian apologetics in a postmodern world.[19] The new emphasis on apologetics as an integral part of the Anglican Communion's corporate response to the Decade of Evangelism will mean an increasing determination to engage with, rather than evade, the realities of human experience. But that attempt will not be based on a fictional belief in "universal human experience." Rather, it will recognize the particularity of experience and develop people-centered approaches that reflect this.[20] For such reasons, we must insist that experience is to be addressed, interpreted and transformed in the light of the gospel proclamation of redemption through Christ, as this is made known to us through Scripture and the Christian tradition. By thus anchoring theology in the bedrock of divine revelation, while linking it to the world of human experience, we may ensure that Christian theology remains both authentic and relevant in the years that lie ahead. Theology can address experience, without becoming reduced to the level of a mere reiteration of what we experience and observe.

For such reasons, the second approach mentioned earlier to the understanding of the relation between experience and theology has regained a hearing.

Theology Interprets Experience

According to the second approach, Christian theology provides a framework by which the ambiguities of experience may be interpreted. It is like a net that we can cast over experience in order to capture its meaning. Experience is seen as something that is to be interpreted, rather than something that is itself capable of interpreting. Christian theology thus aims to *address*, *interpret* and *transform* human experience. Experience is seen as the *interpretandum*, rather than the *interpretans*, that which is to be interpreted rather than something which itself is capable of interpreting other issues. In what follows, I propose to explore these themes with particular reference to the writings of Martin Luther and Clive Staples (Jack) Lewis, best known to his many readers as C. S. Lewis, one of Anglicanism's most influential theologians. These writers indicate the enormous potential of a theology that is able to address, yet not be reduced to, human experience.

Theology Addresses Experience

Christian theology cannot remain faithful to its subject matter if it regards itself as purely propositional or cognitive in nature. The Christian encounter with God is transformative. As Søren Kierkegaard pointed out in his *Unscientific Postscript*, to know the truth is to be known by the truth. "Truth" is something that affects our inner being, as we become involved in "an appropriation process of the most passionate inwardness."[21] This is in no sense to deny or to deemphasize the cognitive aspects of Christian theology. It is merely to observe that there is more to theology than cerebralized information. A theology that touches the mind, leaving the heart unaffected, is no true Christian theology.

This point is stressed by Martin Luther, a theologian who has had a massive impact on modern theology at this point.[22] Although Luther is critical of the role of experience in spirituality, he does not dismiss it as an irrelevance. Indeed, Luther insists that there is one experience that is basic to being a theologian. He describes this briefly in one of his most quoted (and most difficult) statements. "It is living, dying and even being condemned that makes a theologian – not reading, speculating and understanding."[23] When I first read these words of Luther, I found them baffling. Surely theology was about reading Scripture and trying to make sense of it. What was Luther complaining about? Now I know, and I am convinced that Luther is right. To be a *real* theologian is to wrestle with none other than the living God – not with ideas about God, but with God himself. And how can a sinner ever hope to deal adequately with this God?

If you want to be a real theologian, Luther insists, you must have experienced a sense of condemnation. You must have had a moment of insight, in which you realize just how sinful you really are and how much you merit the condemnation of God. Christ's death on the cross spells out the full extent of God's wrath against sin and shows us up as ones who are condemned. It is only from this point that we can fully appreciate the central theme of the New Testament – how God was able to deliver sinners from their fate. Without a full awareness of our sin and the dreadful gulf this opens up between ourselves and God, we cannot appreciate the joy and wonder of the proclamation of forgiveness through Jesus Christ. In a letter to his colleague Philip Melanchthon, dated 13 January 1522, Luther suggested that he ask the so-called prophets who were then confusing the faithful at Wittenberg the following question: "Have they experienced spiritual distress and the divine birth, death and hell?" A list of spiritual sensations is no substitute for the terror that accompanies a real encounter with the living God. For these modern prophets, Luther wrote, "the sign of the Son of man is missing."

Just about anyone can read the New Testament and make some sort of sense of it. But, Luther insists, the *real* theologian is someone who has experienced a sense of condemnation on account of sin – who reads the New Testament and realizes that the message of forgiveness is good news for him or her. The gospel is thus experienced as something liberating, something that transforms our situation, something that is relevant to us. It is very easy to read the New Testament as if it were nothing more than any other piece of literature. And Luther reminds us that it is only through being aware of our sin and all its implications, that we can fully appreciate the wonder of the electrifying declaration that God has forgiven our sins through Jesus Christ.

Theology Interprets Experience

It is a consequence of the Christian doctrine of creation that we are made in the image of God. There is an inbuilt capacity – indeed, we might say, an inbuilt *need* – to relate to God. To fail to relate to God is to fail to be completely human. To be fulfilled is to be filled by God. Nothing that is transitory can ever fill this need. Nothing that is not itself God can ever hope to take the place of God. And yet, because of the fallenness of human nature, there is now a natural tendency to try to make other things fulfill this need.

Sin moves us away from God and tempts us to put other things in his place. Created things thus come to be substituted for God. And they do not satisfy. Like the child who experiences and expresses dissatisfaction when the square peg fails to fit the round hole, so we experience a sense of dissatisfaction. Somehow, we are left with a feeling of longing – longing for *something* undefinable, of which human nature knows nothing, save that we do not possess it.

This phenomenon has been recognized since the dawn of human civilization. In one of his dialogues, Plato compares human beings to leaky jars.[24] Somehow, we are always unfulfilled. We may pour things into the containers of our lives, but something prevents them from ever being entirely filled. We are always partly empty and, for that reason, experience a profound awareness of a lack of fullness and happiness. "Those who have endured the void know that they have encountered a distinctive hunger, or emptiness; nothing earthly satisfies it" (Diogenes Allen).[25]

This well-documented feeling of dissatisfaction is one of the most important points of contact for the gospel proclamation. In the first place, that proclamation interprets this vague and unshaped feeling as a longing for *God*. It gives cognitive substance and shape to what would otherwise be an amorphous and unidentified subjective intuition. And in the second, it offers to fulfill it. There is a sense of divine dissatisfaction – not dissatisfaction with God, but a dissatisfaction with all that is not God, that arises from God and that ultimately leads to God.

Perhaps the most familiar statement of this feeling and its theological interpretation may be found in the famous words of Augustine of Hippo: "You have made us for yourself and our hearts are restless until they rest in you."[26] There is a sense of homesickness for someplace we have never visited, an intimation of a far-off land, that attracts us even though we do not know it.

Augustine finds one of his finest recent apologetic interpreters in the writings of a lay Anglican – the Oxford literary critic and theologian C. S. Lewis. Perhaps one of the most original aspects of Lewis's writing is his persistent and powerful appeal to the religious imagination, in developing Augustine's maxim *"desiderium sinus cordis* (longing makes the heart deep)." Like Augustine, Lewis was aware of certain deep human emotions that pointed to a dimension of our existence beyond time and space. There is, Lewis suggested, a deep and intense feeling of longing within human beings, that no earthly object or experience can satisfy. Lewis terms this sense "joy" and argues that it points to God as its source and goal (hence the title of his celebrated autobiography, *Surprised by Joy*). Joy, according to Lewis, is "an unsatisfied desire which is itself more desirable than any other satisfaction . . . anyone who has experienced it will want it again."[27] But what those this experience *mean*? What, if anything, did it point to?

Lewis addressed this question in a remarkable sermon entitled "The Weight of Glory," preached before the University of Oxford on 8 June 1941. Lewis spoke of "a desire which no natural happiness will satisfy," "a desire, still wandering and uncertain of its object and still largely unable to see that object in the direction where it really lies." There is something self-defeating about human desire, in that what is desired, when achieved, seems to leave the desire unsatisfied. Lewis illustrates this from the age-old quest for beauty, using recognizably Augustinian imagery:

> The books or the music in which we thought the beauty was located will betray us if we trust to them; it was not in them, it only came *through* them and what came through them was longing. These things – the beauty, the memory of our own past – are good images of what we really desire; but if they are mistaken for the thing itself they turn into dumb idols, breaking the hearts of their worshippers. For they are not the thing itself; they are only the scent of a flower we have not found, the echo of a tune we have not heard, news from a country we have not visited.[28]

Human desire, the deep and bittersweet longing for something that will satisfy us, points beyond finite objects and finite persons (who seem able to fulfill this desire, yet eventually prove incapable of doing so); it points *through* these objects and persons toward their real goal and fulfilment in God himself. It is as if human love points to something beyond it, as a parable.

Pleasure, beauty, personal relationships: all seem to promise so much and yet when we grasp them, we find that what we were seeking was not located in them, but lies beyond them. There is a "divine dissatisfaction" within human experience, that prompts us to ask whether there is anything that may satisfy the human quest to fulfill the desires of the human heart. Lewis argues that there is. Hunger, he suggests, is an excellent example of a human sensation that corresponds to a real physical need. This need points to the existence of food by which it may be met. Simone Weil echoes this theme and points to its apologetic importance when she writes: "The danger is not lest the soul should doubt whether there is any bread, but lest, by a lie, it should persuade itself that it is not hungry. It can only persuade itself of this by lying, for the reality of its hunger is not a belief, it is a certainty."[29]

Thirst, according to Lewis, is a further example of a human longing pointing to a human need, that in turn points to its fulfillment in drinking – if the human being in question is to survive. Any human longing, he argues, points to a genuine human need, that in turn points to a real object corresponding to that need. Therefore, Lewis suggests, it is reasonable to suggest that the deep human sense of infinite longing that cannot be satisfied by any physical or finite object or person must point to a real human need that can, in some way, be met. Lewis argues that this sense of longing points to its origin and its fulfillment in God himself.

Lewis's critics argued that his argument rested on an elementary fallacy. Being hungry did not prove that there was bread at hand. The feeling of hunger did not necessarily correspond to a supply of food. This objection, Lewis replied, missed the point.

> A man's physical hunger does not prove that man will get any bread; he may died of starvation in a raft in the Atlantic. But surely a man's hunger does prove that he comes of a race which repairs its body by eating and inhabits a world where eatable substances exist. In the same way, though I do not believe (I wish I did) that my desire for Paradise proves that I shall enjoy it, I think it a pretty good indication that such a thing exists and that some men will. A man may love a woman and not win her; but it would be very odd if the phenomenon called "falling in love" occurred in a sexless world.[30]

Theology thus interprets human experience. Yet at times, experience needs to be radically *re*interpreted. This is a major theme of Luther's "theology of the cross."[31] For Luther, the cross mounts a powerful attack on another human resource upon which too much spiritual weight is often placed, especially in modern Western thought. The experience of the individual is singled out as having revelatory authority. "What I experience is what is right." "Personally, I don't experience it that way." Luther suggests that individual experience is often seriously unreliable as a guide to matters of faith. The way we experience things isn"t necessarily the way things really are.

An example – which I hasten to add is not used by Luther

himself – might be helpful in bringing out the point at issue. Suppose you have been out of doors for some time on a very cold night. You arrive at the house of a friend, who notices how cold you are. "What you need is a good drink," he tells you. "Have a glass of brandy." You drink it, and after a few minutes, you become conscious of a feeling of warmth. You experience the brandy as having warmed you.

But in fact, the brandy will make you colder. The alcohol causes your blood vessels to dilate, giving you the impression that your body is *producing* heat; actually, it is *losing* heat. You may feel that you are warming up; in reality, you are cooling down. Heat is being given off from your body, not taken in by it. Your feelings have led you seriously astray. Were you to drink alcohol to "warm yourself up" in a bitterly cold situation, it is quite possible you could die from the resulting heat loss. An external observer would be able to detect what was really happening, but this perspective would be denied to you, to the extent that you relied upon your feelings.

This example has real theological relevance. It makes the point that experience needs to be *criticized*. You *felt* that you were being warmed up, but the correct interpretation of that experience is that you actually felt the heat leaving your body, to be radiated outward and lost to you. You need an external reference point by which those feelings can be evaluated and judged. Luther develops a related argument: our experiences of God need to be interpreted. The way we experience things is not necessarily the way things really are. The cross provides an external reference point by which our feelings can be evaluated and judged.

Perhaps the best way to understand the spiritual importance of Luther's approach here is to consider the scene of helplessness and hopelessness on that first Good Friday, as Jesus Christ died on the cross. The crowd gathering round the cross were expecting something dramatic to happen. If Jesus really was the son of God, they could expect God to intervene and rescue him. Yet, as that long day wore on, there was no sign of a dramatic divine intervention. In his cry from the cross, even Jesus himself

81

experienced a momentary yet profound sense of the absence of God: "My God, my God, why have you forsaken me?" Many expected God to intervene dramatically in the situation, to deliver the dying Jesus. But nothing of the kind happened. Jesus suffered and finally died. There was no sign of God acting in that situation. So those who based their thinking about God solely on experience drew the obvious conclusion: God was not there.

The resurrection overturned that judgment. God was revealed as having been present and active at Calvary, working out the salvation of humanity and the vindication of Jesus Christ. He was not *perceived* to be present – but present he really was. What experience interpreted as the *absence* of God, the resurrection showed as the *hidden presence* of God. God may have been experienced as inactive, yet the resurrection showed God to have been active behind the scenes, working in secret. For Luther, the resurrection demonstrates how unreliable the verdict of human experience really is. Instead of relying on the misleading impressions of human experience, we should trust in God's promises. God promises to be present with us, even in life's darkest hours – and if experience cannot detect him as being present, then that verdict of experience must be considered unreliable.

Theology Transforms Experience

Christian theology does not simply address the human situation; it offers to transform it. We are not simply told that we are sinners, in need of divine forgiveness and renewal; that forgiveness and renewal is offered to us in the gospel proclamation. If the negative aspect of the Christian proclamation of the crucified Christ is that we are far from God, the positive side is that he offers to bring us home to him through the death and resurrection of his Son. Theology, then, does not simply interpret our experience in terms of alienation from God. It addresses that experience, interprets it as a sign of our global alienation from God through sin and offers to transform it through the grace of God.

One of the many merits of the writings of C. S. Lewis is that

82

they take seriously the way in which words can *generate* and *transform* experience. In his autobiography *Surprised by Joy*, he comments on the effect of a few lines of poetry on his imagination. The lines are from Longfellow's *Saga of King Olaf*:

> I heard a voice that cried,
> Balder the beautiful
> Is dead, is dead.

These words had a profound impact upon the young Lewis, as he later reflected.

> I knew nothing about Balder; but instantly I was uplifted into huge regions of northern sky, I desired with almost sickening intensity something never to be described (except that it is cold, spacious, severe, pale and remote) and then . . . found myself at the very same moment already falling out of that desire and wishing I were back in it.[32]

Words, Lewis thus discovered, have the ability to evoke an experience we have not yet had, in addition to describing an experience we are familiar with. What is known functions as a pointer to that which is yet to be known and that lies within our grasp. In his essay *The Language of Religion*, Lewis made this crucial point using the analogy of a map that points beyond its bounds to what lies beyond it:

> This is the most remarkable of the powers of Poetic language: to convey to us the quality of experiences which we have not had, or perhaps can never have, to use factors within our experience so that they become pointers to something outside our experience – as two or more roads on a map show us where a town that is off the map must lie. Many of us have never had an experience like that which Wordsworth records near the end of *Prelude* XIII; but when he speaks of "the visionary dreariness," I think we get an inkling of it.[33]

At its best, Christian theology shares this characteristic of poetic language (not *poetry* itself, incidentally, Lewis stresses, but the *language used in poetry*), as identified by Lewis: it tries to convey to us the quality of the Christian experience of God. It attempts to point beyond itself, to rise above itself, straining at its lead as it rushes ahead, to point us to a town beyond its map – a town it knows is there, but to which it cannot lead us.

Theology is able to use words in such a way as to offer some pointers for the benefit of those who have yet to discover what it feels like to experience God. It uses a cluster of key words to try to explain what it is like to know God, by analogy with words associated with human experience. It is like forgiveness; in other words, if you can imagine what it feels like to be forgiven for a really serious offense, you can begin to understand the Christian experience of forgiveness. It is like reconciliation; if you can imagine the joy of being reconciled to someone who matters very much to you, you can get a glimpse of what the Christian experience of coming home to God is like. It is like coming home after being away and alone for a long time and perhaps fully expecting never to be able to return. Apologetics uses analogies like these to try to point the way, like roads leading off Lewis's map to an unseen town, to the Christian experience of God, for the benefit of those who have yet to have this transforming experience.

But how is theology able to use words in this way? Is there not a certain arbitrariness to this whole business? How can we take the human experience of reconciliation and dare to say that it somehow echoes that of reconciliation with God? It is here that the Christian doctrine of creation undergirds our theological affirmations. The analogy is given, not invented. It is, so to speak, built into the order of things, a theological insight which is undergirded by the doctrine of the "analogy of being", given definitive expression in the writings of Thomas Aquinas. To speak of "redemption," "forgiveness," "reconciliation" or "liberation" is indeed to speak of situations within this human world. But it is also, through the creative grace of God, to speak of the entry of God into his world and his ability to convey himself through our words.[34]

In this chapter, I have suggested that classical Anglicanism has an experiential deficit. Yet it is a deficit that is relatively easily remedied, by drawing upon the Augustinian theological tradition to which Anglicanism, in common with other Western churches, is heir. The legacy of the past turns out to be surprisingly useful in addressing the issues of the present. Engagement with experience does not and should not, entail a break with or a neglect of the Christian theological tradition, that possesses resources upon which the modern church can draw. This naturally leads on to the general issue of "returning to roots," that has become so important a feature of Western culture in general and theology in particular.[35] With its deep sense of historical roots, Anglicanism is naturally placed to benefit from this development. Any program of theological renewal within Anglicanism will include reference to this theme of "recollecting roots," as discussed in chapter 6.

Attention turns now to a question of major importance, that must be addressed before we can consider the theme of theological renewal in any depth. This is the need to reconsider the whole idea of the *via media* or "middle way," that has been so significant a component of Anglican thinking in the last century. There is a need to restructure this approach, in order to address the religious situation of today, rather than that of the sixteenth century.

5

Reconstructing the *Via Media*

The idea of a *via media* has fascinated Anglicans, especially during the nineteenth century.[1] Much has been made of the manner in which the emerging English national church attempted to steer a middle road between Roman Catholicism and Protestantism. The notion of mediation between two extremes has become, for many, a central element of Anglican self-definition. Historically, there is ample evidence to lend weight to this contention. The Elizabethan Settlement (1559) is widely regarded as a studied attempt to steer a middle course between a somewhat conservative Catholicism that had gained the ascendancy during the reign of Mary Tudor and the more radical forms of Protestantism that were attempting to displace it.

The social conditions of England in the 1560s, during which Anglicanism may be argued to have come into being, made any theological precision on the part of the emerging English reformed church undesirable. Faced with the considerable difficulty of achieving a religious settlement in the midst of the instability of the period, Elizabeth I had little stomach for the protracted theological debates that would have been the inevitable prelude to and continuing outcome of a detailed Confession of Faith. Her concern was for religious peace, rather than doctrinal precision and its attendant theological acrimony.[2] The need for doctrinal definition of considerable precision was evident in the case of Germany during the 1550s and 1560s: the coexistence of Lutheran and Roman Catholic communities in contiguous areas of the region led to demands for public criteria of demarcation, by which the rival communities could be distinguished from one another – a pressure that increased still further with the establishment of Calvinism in the Palatinate in the 1560s.[3] No comparable situation existed in England. As Robert Morgan remarks, "in a fairly monolithic Christian culture, cut off by sea from neighbouring states, when Roman Catholics and other nonconformists could be penalized and marginalized, it was possible to maintain a church's boundaries largely by a common liturgy and polity."[4] The Thirty-Nine Articles (1571) are explicitly described as being for "for the avoiding of diversity of opinions and for the establishing of consent touching true religion." They are not and were never intended to be, a confession of faith.[5]

This is not to say that the Articles are a set piece of studied ambiguity; they are, in fact, quite explicit at a number of points, especially when interpreted within their historical context and certainly in the light of the continuing threat posed to the Elizabethan Settlement by a revitalized Roman Catholicism and an increasingly militant Puritan wing within the English church itself. Rather, it is to note that they are minimal in their specifications. The Articles do not commit the reformed English church to anything other than an affirmation of the main points of the catholic faith, allowing a considerable degree of freedom in relation to areas of potential division.

In essence, therefore, the English national church may be seen to have set itself consciously to steer a middle course between Roman Catholicism and Protestantism. Rejecting the view that mediation implies mediocrity, Anglicanism sought to affirm the common faith of the Christian church, grounded in the New Testament and given a particular focus during the first five centuries of Christian history.[6] This approach was characteristic of the mainstream Reformation, which regarded the Middle Ages as a period of gradual accretion and distortion to which the

Reformation itself was a somewhat overdue corrective. Although emphasizing the priority of the New Testament over its interpreters, the mainstream reformers recognized that Scripture had been read and interpreted within the early Christian communities.[7] A radically individualist approach to biblical interpretation, that eventually proved normative for the radical reformers, was rejected in favor of the reading and interpretation of Scripture within the context of a believing historical community of faith.

The popular misrepresentation of the Reformation as marking a break with the historical past of the church, or a refusal to come to terms with the living tradition of the church, is at variance with the facts. The reformers had no intention of founding a new church; they were concerned to renew and reform an existing church. The imperial politics of the sixteenth century eventually led to them being forced outside the institutional church of the time; this was not, however, their intention. The reformers saw themselves as creating a reforming and renewing *ecclesiola in ecclesia*, maintaining continuity with the *fons et origo* of Christian tradition in the New Testament and, subsequently, in the patristic period. Philip Melanchthon typifies this approach, in his assertion that the Reformation was fundamentally a return to the ideas of Ambrose and Augustine, as much as it was a return to Scripture.[8] The fundamental coinherence of both Scripture and the early Christian proclamation is a major theme of both Lutheran and Reformed writers during the later sixteenth century and makes its appearance in many early seventeenth-century Anglican writings.[9]

The traditional idea of a *via media* has much to commend it. Nevertheless, things have changed. Denominational distinctives are increasingly being seen as of minor importance in relation to other issues that now overshadow them. There is an urgent need for Anglicanism to define itself in relation to two major theological trends that are threatening to tear many churches apart, especially in the West. These tendencies are now generally known as "fundamentalism" and "liberalism." Taken together, they define the acceptable limits within which responsible theology should operate.

It is nothing short of tragic that words should become debased by their associations. The words "fundamentals" and "liberal" both have a real place within the Anglican tradition; indeed, some would even say that they are identity-giving for Anglicans. The former designates a concern for and commitment to the "fundamentals of faith," that Anglicanism shares and proclaims in common with all other Christian churches. Richard Hooker spoke of "these things which supernaturally appertain to the very essence of Christianity and are necessarily required in every particular Christian."[10] The latter refers to the spirit of tolerance and openness that has often been identified as a controlling feature of the Anglican outlook, especially a willingess to "join the world's search for honest answers."[11] Anglican "liberalism," in its classic sense, has taken the form of a studied reluctance to make dogmatic statements and a desire to maintain an openness and toleration – indeed, even a *generosity* – towards a diversity of views. Yet one of the most distressing developments in recent years is the manner in which each of these terms has become tainted. The ideas that they represent – namely, a concern for Christian basics and a generosity of spirit – remain an integral part of the Anglican ethos. Yet the terms that once denoted these qualities now possess very different nuances – nuances that render them intensely problematical in the present day. Each of these tendencies is explored individually in the following sections of this chapter.

Fundamentalism

In 1910, there appeared the first of a series of twelve books from a small American publishing house. The series was unremarkably entitled *The Fundamentals*.[12] Through a sequence of historical accidents, the term "fundamentalist" took its name from this series of works. Fundamentalism arose as a religious reaction within American culture to the rise of a secular culture.[13] Despite the wide use of the term to refer to trends within Islam and Judaism, the term originally and properly designates a movement arising within Protestant Christianity in the United States, especially during the period 1920–40. Yet it is not correct to regard the movement simply as a return to older positions, although aspects of fundamentalist teachings may indeed be discerned in the writings of classic Reformed theologians of the late sixteenth century, or in those of the Old Princeton School, such as Benjamin B. Warfield and Charles Hodge. As James Davison Hunter points out, fundamentalism cannot be equated with "a basic unaltered orthodoxy":

> Orthodoxy as a cultural system represents what could be called a "consensus through time" – more specifically, a consensus based upon the ancient rules and precepts derived from divine revelation. Its authority and legitimacy derive from an unaltering continuity with truth as originally revealed – truth in its primitive and purest expression. *Fundamentalism is orthodoxy in confrontation with modernity.*[14]

Fundamentalism is a deliberate and considered reaction to developments in the twentieth century and is thus, in one sense of the word, thoroughly "modern." It was from its outset and has remained, a counter cultural movement, using central doctrinal affirmations as a means of defining cultural boundaries. Certain central doctrines (most notably, the absolute literal authority of Scripture and the premillennial return of Christ) were treated as barriers, intended as much to alienate secular culture as to give fundamentalists a sense of identity and purpose.[15] A siege mentality became characteristic of the movement; fundamentalist counter communities viewed themselves as walled cities, or (to evoke the pioneer spirit) circles of wagons, defending their distinctive beliefs against an unbelieving culture.[16]

The tendency for radical evangelical movements to separate from an "unbelieving" culture has existed since the sixteenth century. The Radical Reformation, often referred to as "Anabaptism," focused on the need for believers to separate from a godless society and form communities of the committed faithful.[17] The same trend can be seen at many other points in Western religious history – for example, among Baptist communities in seventeenth-century London. Yet the rise of

91

fundamentalism in the United States during the 1920s saw the separatist tendency reach its zenith. The doctrinally pure chose to separate from those who were deemed impure. Perhaps one of the most significant symbols of this trend can be seen in the formation of Westminster Theological Seminary, as a result of a reaction against the alleged "liberalism" of Princeton Theological Seminary at this time.[18] In his influential study *Christ and Culture*, H. Richard Niebuhr characterized this stance as "Christ against Culture."[19] Although Niebuhr finds this model primarily in the period of the early church (especially Tertullian), monasticism and later writers such as Tolstoy, it is clear that one of the unacknowledged targets of his critique of counter-cultural trends is the Anabaptist tradition within American Christianity, that fundamentalism embraced at this point (to the alarm, it has to be said, of many Anabaptist writers).[20]

The emphasis on the premillennial return of Christ is of special significance as a component of this "Christ against Culture" *mentalité*. This view has a long history; it never attained any especial degree of influence prior to the nineteenth century, when it began to gain ground through the writings of J. N. Darby. However, fundamentalism appears to have discerned in the idea an important weapon against the liberal Christian idea of a kingdom of God upon earth, to be achieved through social action. "Dispensationalism," especially of a premillenarian type, became an integral element of fundamentalism. Such dispensationalist views, it must be stressed, have had minimal impact within English evangelicalism of any shape during the twentieth century. As historian David Bebbington comments, fundamentalist controversies existed in Britain during the period between the First and Second World Wars; however, they were "storms in a teacup when compared with the blizzards of invective that swept contemporary America."[21] It appears to have been the Baptists who were most deeply affected by these developments;[22] Anglicanism was not particularly affected. A similar pattern emerges within the Canadian context, where fundamentalist attitudes were of relatively minor importance in shaping the Christian response to the general drift of Canadian culture away from its original Christian moorings.[23] Similarly, Australian evangelicalism has been relatively little influenced by fundamentalist trends, whereas what might be termed "conservative Protestantism" or "classic evangelicalism" has been of major importance since the First World War, especially in the city of Sydney.[24]

The emergence of evangelicalism (or, as it was then known, "neo-evangelicalism") as a distinctive option, avoiding the fatal weaknessses of fundamentalism, dates from the period immediately following the Second World War. Carl F. H. Henry argued that fundamentalists did not present Christianity as a world-view, with a distinctive social vision, but chose to concentrate on only one aspect of the Christian proclamation. As a result, an impoverished and reduced gospel was presented to the world, radically defective in its social vision. Fundamentalism was too other-worldly and antiintellectual to gain a hearing among the educated public and unwilling to concern itself with exploring how Christianity related to culture and social life in general.[25] His *Uneasy Conscience of Modern Fundamentalism* (1947) sounded a clarion call for *cultural engagement* on the part of evangelicals.

As Millard J. Erickson pointed out, it had become increasingly clear that fundamentalism had totally failed to turn back the rising tide of liberalism, that it had not achieved any significant impact on the thought world of its day and that it had spurned the social problems of its time.[26] Initially, the terms "neo-evangelicalism" or "new evangelicalism" were used to refer to this third force in North American Protestantism; gradually, these were displaced by the simpler and more economical term "evangelicalism," distinguished by its stalwart defense of orthodox Christian faith, backed up by solid theological scholarship and its commitment to the social application of the gospel message.[27]

Historians are agreed that "fundamentalism" has never had any significant place within Anglicanism, which has thus largely been spared the traumas that shook the American religious establishment earlier this century. In part, the Anglican ethos has had a significant impact in this matter, in that Anglicanism has had a long tradition of positive interaction with the prevailing culture. In part, this reflects the unusual position of the Church of England, which, as a national church, was under pressure to engage positively with mainline culture. If Western Anglicanism has been prone to any tendency, it has never been that of rejecting mainline culture to form a Christian counterculture; rather, it is that of affirming contemporary culture to a point at which it risks becoming submerged by it.

Evangelicalism, which has come to play a major role in global Anglicanism during the past twenty years, cannot be equated with "fundamentalism," despite the flawed attempt of James Barr, in his *Fundamentalism* (1977), to foster this impression.[28] As Canadian scholar Clark Pinnock observes, "The people Barr is sharply and vehemently criticizing, the British evangelicals, do not like the term being applied to them because they are not, in fact, fundamentalists."[29] Some twenty years ago, historian Richard Quebedeaux complained of the uncritical and hostile tendency of "mainstream ecumenical liberalism to lump together with pejorative intent all theological conservatives into the worn fundamentalist category."[30]

Fundamentalism, then, has few friends inside Anglicanism. Yet it will be obvious that a concern for *fundamentals* does not make one a "fundamentalist." Stephen Sykes, bishop of Ely, is one of a number of writers to have reflected on the role of "fundamental articles" in recent years;[31] none would regard him as a "fundamentalist" for that reason. It is not a concern for "right doctrine" or "fundamental articles of faith" that has attracted such criticism of fundamentalism. It is fundamentalism's refusal to take the scholarly study of Scripture seriously and its persistent antiintellectual bias that have made it so problematical. For its critics, fundamentalism is a visceral reaction to the modern world in general, devoid of any form of critical engagement with modernity. It represents a retreat from the modern world into the safety of a premodern world, without engaging with the issues.

Yet a reaction against the assumptions of the Enlightenment is a major feature of recent thought. Does, perhaps, fundamentalism have a point, after all? Yet it must be noted that there is a world of difference between the postmodern rejection of the Enlightenment because of its fatally flawed intellectual assumptions and the fundamentalist rejection of the Enlightenment because of an emotional dislike of the modernizing agenda of the movement. The former represents a principled and intellectually informed critique of the Enlightenment. The latter represents a gut reaction against it, devoid of any serious intellectual engagement or evaluation.

Yet these considerations raise an important point. There is a tidal wave of dissent rising against the Enlightenment in modern Western culture, given added impetus by a growing cultural critique of the West by the developing world. A commitment to Enlightenment values and ideas is increasingly being criticized as ethnocentric. To reject modernity is thus not in itself the unique prerogative of fundamentalism. Postmodernism and postliberalism are two major movements within the modern academic world that have rejected the Enlightenment approach to religion, especially Christianity. Many movements within the modern church are demanding that we find a better world-view than the narrow and pedantic Enlightenment rationalism that has dominated much academic Christian thinking for the last two centuries. The growing chorus of demand within the churches to return to and rediscover the distinctive features of the Christian tradition cannot be dismissed as "fundamentalist." It represents a desire to return to roots – roots that have been forgotten or deliberately suppressed. This central theme of modern theology is explored in further detail in the following chapter. Attention now turns to the tendency diametrically opposed to fundamentalism – liberalism.

Liberalism

In a sermon preached to commemorate the long and distinguished career of Alan Webster, former dean of St Paul's Cathedral, London, Robert Runcie (then archbishop of Canterbury) commented on how the word "liberal" seemed to have fallen into disrepute. There can be no quarreling with his observation. To refer to a writer as a "liberal" has acquired decidedly negative overtones, almost as great as those attending the use of the word "fundamentalist." This development is not entirely lacking in foundation. It seems that the terms "modernist" and "radical" are gradually falling out of use and their more negative associations are coming to be projected onto "liberalism," a word that was originally innocent of such associations.

One of the greatest tragedies of our times is that in recent years "liberalism" has, in the view of many observers, degenerated from a commitment to openness and toleration into an intolerant and dogmatic world-view, that refuses to recognize the validity of any views save its own. Appropriate here are the words of my distinguished Oxford colleague John Macquarrie, unquestionably one of Anglicanism's greatest living theologians:

> What is meant by "liberal" theology? If it means only that the theologian to whom the adjective is applied has an openness to other points of view, then liberal theologians are found in all schools of thought. But if "liberal" becomes itself a party label, then it usually turns out to be extremely illiberal.[32]

The deeply disturbing paradox of much modern theology – including, it has to be said, Anglican theology – is that some of the most dogmatic of its representatives lay claim to being liberals. Liberalism, in the traditional and honorable sense of the word, carries with it an inalienable respect for and openness to the views of others. The new dogmatism within liberalism is itself a sure indication of a deep sense of unease and insecurity and an awareness of its growing isolation and marginalization within mainline Christianity, Anglicanism included.

Some years ago, Stephen Sykes suggested that liberalism represented a destructive trend within Anglicanism. "Liberalism is a cuckoo in the Anglican nest and the all-too facile inclusion of it under the guise of a 'party' with a long and honoured history in Anglicanism was bound to be no more than a temporary measure."[33] Although some liberal writers have defended the view that liberalism is a party that mediates between evangelicalism and catholicism, almost as a *via media* within a *via media*, it is becoming increasingly clear that this is not the case. "Liberalism" does not represent a point midway on a line drawn between evangelicalism and catholicism; for all its defects, the term *central churchmanship* refers far more accurately to such a mediating position. Evangelicalism and catholicism, as is increasingly being stressed, have far more in common with each other than they do with liberalism, not least their shared commitment to the authority of God's self-revelation in Christ, the uniqueness of Christianity, the divinity of Christ and the historicity of the resurrection.

Sykes's argument rests partly upon the assumption that "liberalism is a negative phenomenon . . . a 'liberal' theological proposal is always in the form of a challenge to an established authority."[34] John Macquarrie points out that this trend has "led to a type of theology which is parasitic, in the sense that it criticizes the tradition but makes no contribution of its own to what ought to be a growing, expanding tradition."[35] If Sykes is correct here, it follows that liberalism is, as Macquarrie suggests, parasitic, in that it defines itself negatively, to the extent that it departs or dissents from other established positions – such as catholicism or evangelicalism. Curiously, the wellbeing of liberalism would thus depend on the prior health of either or both catholicism and evangelicalism, to the extent that it chooses to depart at points from them. If Sykes" analysis is correct – and it remains to be seen whether this is the case – Anglicanism cannot expect renewal through its liberal wing. Anglicanism can only hope to be renewed by either or both its catholic and evangelical wings, from which liberals may choose to distance themselves, to varying degrees.

The origins of the term "liberalism" appear to lie in early Victorian England. By the 1830s, the term "liberal" was in fairly regular use, referring especially to a political attitude that celebrated the cult of personal liberty. In his *Prometheus Unbound*, Shelley wrote of human nature as "free, uncircumscribed, equal, unclassed, tribeless and nationless." Human nature was subject to none and totally free in its choices. Initially, economic, political, and religious liberalism were intertwined; however, as it became increasingly clear that a political or economic revolution would not take place in England, the liberal agenda came to be focused on religious issues. The movement came to be distinguished by its optimism, as seen in John Morley's (1838–1923) famous declaration "that human nature is good, that the world is capable of being made a desirable abiding place and that the evil of the world is the fruit of bad education and bad institutions."[36]

This sentiment can be found in much liberal Anglican thinking of the early twentieth century and was often attributed, on the basis of the rather naive historical positivism that characterized that period, to Jesus himself. James Franklin Bethune-Baker's declaration that "human society has in it the immortal germs of progress towards its perfection and the conditions of its perfectibility were described by such sayings are collected in the Sermon on the Mount"[37] can be seen both as representing this perfectionist view of human nature, while simultaneously illustrating the liberal tendency to project thoroughly modern views onto Jesus – a trend devastatingly caricatured by George Tyrrell, with particular reference to Adolf von Harnack: "The Christ that Harnack sees, looking back through nineteen centuries of catholic darkness, is only the reflection of a liberal Protestant face, seen at the bottom of a deep well."[38] For many, these progressive social ideas were left in tatters in the aftermath of the First and Second World Wars, especially as the horrors of the Nazi extermination camps became widely known. It also illustrates the linkage between "liberalism" and "modernism," that has increasingly proved to be an embarrassment to the former.

Liberalism is now increasingly dismissed as an irrelevance by both conservative and mainline Christian writers, impatient with its easy accommodation to contemporary Western culture and its apparently uncritical abandonment of much that is seen to be of vital importance to Christianity. Its critics charge it with playing to a secular gallery and giving encouragement to an increasingly self-confident anti-Christian tendency in Western culture. The writings of John Shelby Spong are often singled out as a case in point, allegedly demonstrating the intellectual vacuity, the shallow scholarship and the cultural puritanism of this committed and self-consciously liberal approach. The obvious inadequacy of these writings makes the charges of irrelevance and irresponsibility temptingly easy to endorse. Rather than indulge in such a pointless pursuit, I propose to try to identify what it is about liberalism that has caused such a loss of confidence to emerge within the movement.

The liberal approach is at its most realistic and credible within a context in which there is a single outlook characteristic of society as a whole. Sociologist Peter L. Berger notes that "every human society has its own corpus of officially credited wisdom, the beliefs and values that most people take as self-evidently true." There was a point, in both North America and Great Britain, when society was both culturally homogeneous and professedly Christian. In such a context, liberalism had considerable appeal. But this neat and tidy approach has become virtually unworkable by the chronic intellectual and moral pluralism of modern Western society. In the past – for example, in sixteenth-century England – there may only have been only one set of beliefs and values in a culture; now, there are many competing beliefs and values on offer, encouraged by a state polity that has come to regard the tolerance and fostering of plurality as a national goal in itself, consonant with the pursuit of individual liberty.[39]

Liberalism here finds itself increasingly adrift, for two reasons. In the first place, it is a sad fact of life that pluralism, while wishing to encourage toleration, seems also to stimulate emergence of a degree of fanaticism. Critics of contemporary liberalism often cite its intolerance toward rival worldviews as evidence of its problems at this juncture. Sociologically, the issue has become important to modern American society. As Berger observes:

> This pluralistic situation usually forces on people a certain degree of tolerance; but it also sharpens the cognitive dissonances and therefore introduces an element of fanaticism into the quarrel. This co-existence of tolerance and fanaticism is an important characteristic of modern America.[40]

99

The real problem, however, relates to the traditional liberal insistence that Christian theology relate to "modern ways of thinking" or "values acceptable to our culture." In a monolithic and static culture, this poses no problems; however, in a rapidly changing society that is openly committed to pluralism, these demands degenerate into little more than platitudes. *Which* ways of thinking? *Which* values? Philosopher Alasdair MacIntyre, reacting against naive rhetoric about "rationality" and "justice," provocatively entitled his celebrated book, severely undermining liberalism's intellectual foundations, *Whose Justice? Which Rationality?* Furthermore, the rapid pace of cultural change in the West results in cultural accommodation having an inbuilt outdatedness; today's prevailing wisdom rapidly becomes tomorrow's discarded whims.

The force of this difficulty can be seen by perusing the writings of Cambridge theologian Charles Raven (the subject of many gracious allusions and citations in the recent novels of Susan Howatch). No one who reads his works can can fail to be impressed by the manner in which he attempts to achieve a grand synthesis of Christian faith and modern knowledge. Yet that term "modern" needs translating; perhaps the best interpretation might be something along the lines of "the accepted wisdom of Cambridge senior combination rooms in the 1920s." It may seem more than a little churlish to point out that the apparently assured results of "modern knowledge" upon which Raven laid so much emphasis would be discarded by a later generation; the academic world is not immune to changes in fashion and the recognition of the need to discard the apparently assured judgments of earlier generations. It is, however, theologically necessary to emphasize the sheer *provisionality* of "modernity"; what seemed self-evident in the 1920s (and hence appeared to be an ideal foundation and criterion for liberal theology) is today regarded as outmoded and defunct – along with any theologies founded upon and guided by such assumptions.

To the historian of Christian theology in the last fifty or so years, the same pattern may be seen to emerge consistently: the seemingly assured radical positions of the 1960s came to be overturned during the 1980s. For example, the rise of postmodernism reflects the seriously eroded credibility of a universal rationality once regarded as central to "liberal" theological method. The noted Jewish liberal writer Eugene B. Borowitz is a perceptive critic of this fatally vulnerable trend in liberal theology. Surveying the ruins of liberal religious thought, both Jewish and Christian, Borowitz points out the vulnerability – indeed, the *indefensibility* – of its central beliefs:

> Liberalism lost its cultural hegemony largely because of the demythologization of its allies, universal rationalism and science. At one time we thought them not only our finest sources of truth but our surest means to human ennoblement. Today the sophisticated know that they deal only in possible "constructions of reality" and the masses sense that they commend ethical relativism more than necessary values and duties.[41]

Many liberal writers have emphasized the importance of relating Christianity to its intellectual environment. Yet it must be noted that a concern for the intellectual climate in which Christianity finds itself at any moment is not a unique, or indeed even a *defining*, feature of liberalism. Thomas Aquinas took seriously the Aristotelianism of the thirteenth-century University of Paris in writing both his *Summa contra Gentiles* and *Summa Theologia*. I have yet to find Aquinas described as a liberal for that reason. In fact, this approach is characteristic of reflective and intellectually responsible Christianity through the ages. It has a distinguished presence and history within Anglicanism, in writers as diverse as Richard Hooker, Bishop Butler, John Henry Newman and William Temple. Indeed, one might almost say that this concern, while not being the exclusive monopoly of Anglicanism, is nevertheless one of its hallmarks. For example, it is abundantly clear that Hooker's apologetics, especially his justification of the royal supremacy in state and church, is deeply grounded in an awareness of the contemporary "intellectual climate."[42] Yet Hooker

101

is not a "liberal" writer for that reason; nor would he be thought of as a "liberal" theologian, as that term is now understood. Such an outlook is characteristic of thoughtful Christian reflection over two thousand years of its history, not the exclusive or defining characteristic of "liberalism."

A more modern example will make this point unequivocally clear. One of the most significant contributions to the modern philosophy of religion comes from a group of American writers, including Alvin Plantinga and Nicholas Wolterstorff. Their discussion of the theme of "faith and rationality" has become a landmark in recent debates centring on this theme.[43] Yet the group has no inclination whatsoever toward liberalism, representing instead what one might call the "classic Reformed approach," drawing its inspiration from the writings of John Calvin. In short: there is nothing distinctively "liberal" about being academically serious and culturally informed.

Such sociological and philosophical critiques of liberalism and growing anxiety concerning its pastoral viability, are reflected and reinforced in the writings of Peter L. Berger, one of North America's most distinguished sociologists. Berger comments thus on the enormous difficulties facing the liberal theological enterprise in a modern Western pluralist culture:

> The various efforts by Christians to accommodate to the "wisdom of the world" in this situation becomes a difficult, frantic and more than a little ridiculous affair. Each time that one has, after an enormous effort, managed to adjust the faith to the prevailing culture, that culture turns around and changes. . . . Our pluralistic culture forces those who would "update" Christianity into a state of permanent nervousness. The "wisdom of the world," which is the standard by which they would modify the religious tradition, varies from one social location to another; what is worse, even in the same locale it keeps on changing, often rapidly.[44]

Berger's sociological analysis makes it clear that some views will be "the accepted wisdom in one social milieu and utter

102

foolishness in another." Or, to put it another way, it is not a
universal way of thinking or set of values; it is socially located, in
a specific class or social group. Earlier, it was noted how
"fundamentalism" is often linked with a sociological address that
would look something like "lower middle class from the deep
South." Liberalism has traditionally occupied a rather different
sociological address: that of the cultural élite. Berger's perceptive
comments here merit close study:

> *The wisdom of the world today always has a sociological
> address.* In consequence, every accommodation to it on the
> part of Christians will be "relevant" in one very specific social
> setting (usually determined by class) and "irrelevant" in
> another. Christians, then, who set out to accommodate the
> faith to the modern world should ask themselves which sector
> of that world they seek to address. Very probably, whatever
> *aggiornamento* they come up with will include some, exclude
> others. And if the *aggiornamento* is undertaken with the
> cultural élite in mind, then it is important to appreciate that the
> beliefs of this particular group are the most fickle of all.[45]

It is thus potentially meaningless to talk about "making Christianity
relevant to the modern world." This implies a theoretical
universality to "the modern world" which is absent in reality.
Every attempt to accommodate Christianity to the beliefs of one
social grouping proves to make it irrelevant to another. The
paradox underlying the entire liberal enterprise is that for everyone
for whom the gospel is made "relevant," there is someone else for
whom it is made irrelevant.

The need to be sensitive and responsive to developments within
society is beyond dispute. Nevertheless, to its critics, liberalism
appears to have been possessed of a willingness to allow its agenda
and the resources it brings to bear upon that agenda to be shaped
by transient, nonuniversal cultural trends. The French sociologist
Jacques Ellul identifies this trend, that appears to have reached its
zenith in the late 1960s and early 1970s and notes its fundamental
flaws.

> What troubles me is not that the opinions of Christians change, nor that their opinions are shaped by the problems of the times; on the contrary, that is good. What troubles me is that Christians conform to the trend of the moment without introducing into it *anything* specifically Christian. Their convictions are determined by their social milieu, not by faith in revelation; they lack the uniqueness which ought to be the expression of that faith. Thus theologies become mechanical exercises that justify the positions adopted and justify them on grounds that are absolutely not Christian.[46]

Ellul here puts his finger on one of the most worrying aspects of liberalism during the 1960s: its tendency to fashion theologies in order to justify decisions that have been made on other grounds. Radical new theologies – *radical* being a word that then ensured the cultural credibility of the ideas attached to it – were fashioned, generally with minimal or highly selective reference to the Christian tradition, that provided *post hoc* rationalizations of attitudes and ideas, whose ultimate origin lay firmly in the social milieu. To many, it seemed that liberal theology was little more than a transient agglomerate of ideas and values, deriving primarily from the social milieu in which liberal writers were based – usually universities, detached from the pastoral and social concerns of ordinary lay Christians and increasingly dominated by a secular outlook that theology was expected to share, if it were to maintain any "academic credibility." Liberalism slipped easily from being the addresser to being the addressee of a secular culture.

In their *American Mainline Religion: Its Changing Shape and Future*, sociologists Wade Clark Roof and William McKinney provide an important study of the steady numerical decline in mainline churches, including the Episcopal Church.[47] Yet the importance of the book does not lie merely in its documentation of trends, confirmed by survey after survey and noted in an earlier chapter of this book. Roof and McKinney look ahead to the future and ask what the outcome of these developments will be. Their conclusion? In the 1990s, the challenge to mainline Christianity will not be from "the conservatives it has spurned, but from the secularists it has spawned."[48]

There is an urgent need for liberalism to subject itself to the kind of criticism that fundamentalism went through in the 1940s. A growing number of individuals within the ranks of fundamentalism, especially Carl F. H. Henry, then became convinced that the movement was out of touch with the real world. Henry's program of reformation and renewal – that initially led to the development of "neo-evangelicalism" – is widely regarded as having brought about the kind of changes that were needed if the movement was to retain any kind of intellectual credibility and pastoral relevance. This involved the conscious rejection of both the "fundamentalist" label and its associated theology. We have now reached this stage with liberalism. There is much that is right with liberalism – but that has become overshadowed through its failures and excesses during the 1960s and 1970s, that still linger on into the 1990s. It needs a liberal Carl Henry to see it through this process of self-criticism and self-examination. The rise of postliberalism, especially associated with Yale Divinity School and Duke University Divinity School, may well turn out to represent precisely this process of reappraisal that liberalism so clearly needs. One possible figure who could act as a rallying point for this process of reconsideration within Anglicanism is John Habgood, archbishop of York, widely regarded as one of the finest minds within the Church of England. It is clear that he reflects the kind of liberalism that deserves to have a continuing place in Anglicanism. It is beyond doubt that Habgood has both the academic credentials and pastoral concerns that make him an ideal focus for this process of reconsideration. In many ways, Habgood's vision of liberalism corresponds to the classic liberal catholic vision set out a century ago in *Lux Mundi*. Habgood himself uses the term "conservative liberal" to describe his particular approach and there is much to commend this.[49]

Habgood is unquestionably correct when he suggests that "a constant feature of liberalism is the wish to take seriously the intellectual climate in which faith has to be lived."[50] The issue is that of engagement with modern culture. At no point does

Habgood give any indication of a wish to capitulate to that culture; rather, his concern is apologetic. Christianity is under an obligation to gain a hearing within modern culture; to do so, it must understand that culture and learn to address its concerns in terms that it can understand. As Habgood is at pains to point out, the issue here is not that of capitulating to the world, nor of providing a smokescreen or cloak for a loss of faith in God, but that of *engagement*.

> This is not the same as following intellectual fashion. At the frontiers of academic conversation there obviously has to be an engagement with ideas which are currently in vogue. Much theological writing at this level, like any other writing, tends to be ephemeral and is only dangerously misleading if it is assumed at that instant to express the faith of the church. But underneath such temporary eddies there are much more enduring ground swells . . . Serious liberalism does not start reconstructing its theology at the first hint of secular change . . . But it needs to take seriously the questions posed by fundamental sea-changes and be ready to live with loose ends, partial insights and a measure of agnosticism, without losing its grip on the essentials of faith.[51]

One can have nothing but respect for this "serious liberalism," that has been and ought to be a central element of Anglican self-understanding. This is liberalism in its classic form, concerned for an engagement with the world and a generosity toward all sincerely engaged in the theological enterprise. But, sadly, it is no longer typical of modern "liberalism" as a whole, as that movement has developed recently. In a significant discussion of the development of English theology, Adrian Hastings contrasts the theology of Charles Gore, William Temple, Arthur Michael Ramsey and Austin Farrer with that of Dennis Nineham, John Hick and Don Cupitt. The theology of the former, he remarks, "was, most certainly, one the church could live and thrive with. The same cannot be said for that of Nineham, Hick or Cupitt."[52] There is a real and urgent need for liberalism to go through a sustained process of self-examination in the years ahead. Anglicanism could well provide a matrix within which this process of reconsideration could take place.

Reconstructing the Via Media

In the foregoing discussion, I have deliberately set up a contrast between two tendencies within Christianity. I have not referred to them as "doctrines" or "ideologies," in that the movements are better characterized by their general methods and outlooks, than by the specific doctrines that result from them. On the one hand, there is a tendency that refuses pointblank to engage with contemporary culture and takes refuge in simplistic repetition of the certainties of yesteryear – whether through a somewhat superficial reading of Scripture, or an uncritical appeal to the decisions of the church. On the other, there is a relativizing tendency that treats contemporary cultural values and outlooks – or "common human experience" – as normative, despite all the problems just noted and aims to accommodate Christian insights to them. Anglicanism, by virtue of its social roots and cultural history, has been influenced to a significantly greater extent by this latter tendency. Yet Anglicanism cannot afford to restrict itself to the sociological niches occupied by either fundamentalism or liberalism. It needs to regain its sense of being a *catholic* church, unfettered by the prevailing social conventions of class and culture.

It is now clear that both tendencies have little to contribute to the well-being of Christianity in the West, partly because of the intellectual and spiritual deficiencies of their outlooks, partly because of the specificity and transience of their "sociological addresses" (Peter L. Berger), and partly because of the sharply polemical and divisive strategies they have chosen to deploy in advancing their fortunes. The situation has now become polarized to such an extent that "fundamentalism" has become little more than a polemical term for orthodoxy and "liberalism" for toleration, on the part of those in both camps who wish to discredit alternative positions through the dangerous strategy of "heresy by association."

107

The grave consequences of this polarization can be seen especially painfully from the history of the Presbyterian churches in the United States earlier this century.[53] In 1922, an ill-tempered controversy broke out, that is widely regarded as having marked the beginning of the spiral of numerical decline within that church, laid the foundations of schism within it and ultimately caused a radical loss of theological vision that eroded its distinctiveness within the American situation.

On 21 May 1922, Henry Emerson Fosdick preached a polemical sermon entitled "Shall the Fundamentalists Win?," of which 130,000 copies, rewritten by a skilled public relations expert and funded by John D. Rockefeller Jr., were circulated. A vigorous riposte soon followed. Clarence Edward Macartney entitled his reply "Shall Unbelief Win?." The situation rapidly polarized. Toleration proved impossible. There could be no compromise or way out of the situation. Presbyterians were forced to decide whether they were "unbelieving liberals" or "reactionary fundamentalists." The church was shattered. There were other options and saner voices; the climate of opinion made it impossible for them to gain a hearing.

The Anglican church has never had to face such a devastating controversy in such a radically polarized manner. It is cheap and easy to criticize the traditional Anglican emphasis on "toleration" and "comprehensiveness." The Episcopal Church in the United States, for example, has been described fondly as the "roomiest church in Christendom"[54] on account of its expansively generous and tolerant attitudes towards the theological views of its clergy. Yet this pragmatic approach, so easily criticized as amounting to little more than an absence of doctrinal commitment or a free-floating relativism,[55] has genuinely positive virtues in this context, that must be appreciated. For the same "modernism" that came close to destroying the Presbyterian church in the United States was a genuinely important force within the Church of England during the same period.[56] The Churchmen's Union was founded in 1898 for the advancement of liberal religious thought; in 1928, it altered its name to the Modern Churchmen's Union. Among those especially associated with this group may be noted Kirsopp Lake (1872–1946), E. W. Barnes (1874–1953), Hastings Rashdall (1858–1924), H. D. A. Major (1871–1961) and William R. Inge (1860–1954). The journal *Modern Churchman*, founded in 1911 by Major, served as an organ for the views of the group.

Rashdall's *Idea of Atonement in Christian Theology* (1919) illustrates the general tenor of English modernism. Drawing somewhat uncritically on the earlier writings of the leading nineteenth-century German liberal Protestant theologian A. B. Ritschl, Rashdall argued that the theory of the atonement associated with the medieval writer Peter Abelard was more acceptable to modern thought forms than traditional theories that made an appeal to the notion of a substitutionary sacrifice of Christ. This strongly moral or exemplarist theory of the atonement, that interpreted Christ's death virtually exclusively as a demonstration of the love of God, made a considerable impact on English and especially Anglican, thought in the 1920s and 1930s.[57] The conference of Modern Churchmen, held at Girton College Cambridge, 8–15 August 1921, created a minor sensation, perhaps out of proportion to what was actually said. In its aftermath, pressures as great as those that so distressed the American Presbyterian church began to build up, in the full glare of publicity in both the church and secular press. Yet they were contained within the church.

In the United States, it is clear that modernist trends of the kind just noted were also present in the Episcopal Church. At the 1919 Church Congress, John Wallace Suter (1859–1942) declared his belief that the entire church was ready for "modernist revisions in doctrine." In 1923, Percy Stickney Grant (1860–1927) spoke from his pulpit, in a much-publicized sermon, of the person of Christ in terms that seemed to deny his divinity (the parallels with the Girton conference of 1921 are interesting). Yet the Episcopal Church managed to contain these controversies without schism, living through to another day in which those same struggles could be seen, with the benefit of hindsight, to be less significant than was immediately obvious.

109

The same perspective emerged in England. In December 1922, the Church of England set up a Doctrine Commission, with a membership held to be representative of the Anglo-Catholic, evangelical, and liberal schools of thought. It did not report until 1938; its generally liberal tone caused some excitement at the time, before the outbreak of the Second World War moved minds on to deal with other issues. "It was," according to Adrian Hastings, "a pondered, rather dull document . . . Its better parts reflect the new catholicizing trends to be found in [A. M.] Ramsey; most of the rest is – for the late 1930s – rather anachronistically liberal and modernist. It decided nothing, stimulated little."[58] Ungenerous though that judgment may seem, given the benefit of due historical perspective, it must be noted that there is some truth in its strictures. Yet that Commission's report also prevented the church from fragmenting into "fundamentalist" and "liberal" factions, allowing it to more or less cohere until theological trends such as those outlined in A. M. Ramsey's *Gospel and the Catholic Church* (1936) allowed a process of reconstruction to begin. *The Gospel and the Catholic Church* is itself an important contribution to the kind of *via media* that is now required. Although one of Ramsey's concerns was to mediate between what might be called "Protestant" and "Catholic" tendencies within the church, his book also represented a move toward establishing a new normative center for Anglicanism, that avoids the excesses of both what would now be termed "fundamentalism" and "liberalism."

The one threatens to isolate Christianity from the world; the other, to make Christianity indistinguishable from the world. There must be a means of resolving this impasse between two totally opposed ways of conceiving Christianity. There is a real need for the reconstruction of a *via media* that avoids the increasingly outmoded dialectic between "Catholic" and "Protestant" and addresses the *real* issue of today: the failure of both liberalism and fundamentalism to provide a relevant and responsible form of Christianity for today's world. One collapses into the world, the other refuses to have anything to do with it. If ever a *via media* was needed, it is now. As Hans Küng pointed out recently, the church "must find a way between a modernism without foundations and a fundamentalism without modernity."[59] Anglicanism is poised to provide exactly such a middle way – not as something that has been artificially devised as an expedient compromise between two extremes, but a natural and organic synthesis, grounded in a long history of engagement with the Christian tradition on the one hand and contemporary culture on the other, that affords the means of addressing this vital issue.

The point I wish to stress is simple, yet of fundamental importance. Anglicanism already possesses a concern both for the fundamentals of faith, without being "fundamentalist" and for generous toleration, without being "liberal," as those two terms are now widely understood. Again, I stress how utterly tragic it is that two such honorable terms have become debased; however, we cannot now ignore their negative associations for so large a part of the Christian churches. At least in the short term, the history of memory is irreversible.

Yet precisely that concern for fundamentals and generosity are already integral parts of the Anglican tradition. Here is an already existing *via media* – not a solution that was artificially constructed to solve this problem, but an established ethos, reflecting a settled form of Christian living, that happens to coincide with a major need within the Christian churches. Yale theologian and Episcopal priest Hans Frei used the phrase "a generous orthodoxy" in a related context.[60]

Fundamentalism, in either its traditional Protestant or Catholic forms, is not a viable option for Anglicanism, as it confronts the future. We are not going to get anywhere by running away from the modern world and burying our heads in the consoling sand of the past. For historical reasons, liberalism has had and continues to have a far greater influence on Anglicanism than fundamentalism. In a book written for Anglicans, denouncing fundamentalism would be like preaching to the choir. The weaknesses of the movement are so evident that there is little to be gained through identifying and criticizing them.

Fundamentalism has never been a significant temptation for

Anglicanism. Liberalism, on the other hand, has held considerable attractions for many Western Anglicans, especially in the 1960s and 1970s. Yet liberalism is now widely recognized to have failed – failed to convince its increasingly numerous and articulate critics of both its intellectual credentials and its spiritual relevance. It is out of favor with the academics and it never really appealed much to ordinary churchgoers anyway. If I could give a personal illustration, I myself went through a period (*c.* 1976–82) in which I found myself strongly attracted to the liberal vision, which I believed had both pastoral relevance and intellectual credibility. Yet over a period of years I found my confidence fatally eroded on both counts, an experience of waning confidence that I have now found to be common among my peers around this time.[61]

In the wake of this general collapse of confidence in liberalism there has arisen a new approach, that is receiving careful attention from younger theologians world-wide and holds considerable potential for the future of Anglicanism. This movement, now generally known as "postliberalism," is explored in the following paragraphs. As the name suggests, the movement self-consciously regards itself as an alternative to liberalism, tracing its origins to the aftermath of the collapse in confidence in the theological resources upon which liberalism placed such weight.[62]

Building upon the work of philosophers such as Alasdair MacIntyre, postliberalism rejects both the traditional Enlightenment appeal to a "universal rationality" and the liberal assumption of an immediate religious experience common to all humanity. Arguing that all thought and experience is historically and socially mediated, postliberalism bases its theological program on a return to religious traditions whose values are inwardly appropriated. Postliberalism is thus antifoundational (in that it rejects the notion of a universal foundation of knowledge), communitarian (in that it appeals to the values, experiences, and language of a community, rather than prioritizing those of the individual) and historicist (in that it insists upon the importance of traditions and their associated historical communities in the shaping of experience and thought). In all these respects it moves away from the outmoded assumptions of liberalism, while remaining far removed from the intellectually untenable outlook of fundamentalism.

The most significant statement of the postliberal agenda remains George Lindbeck's *Nature of Doctrine* (1984), discussed in chapter 4. Lindbeck, Pitkin Professor of Historical Theology at Yale Divinity School, rejects liberal "experiential-expressive" theories of doctrine as failing to take account of both human experiential diversity and the mediating role of culture in human thought and experience. In its place, he develops a "cultural-linguistic" approach, which embodies the leading features of postliberalism.[63] This approach denies that there is some universal unmediated human experience that exists apart from human language and culture. Rather, it stresses that the heart of religion lies in living within a specific historical religious tradition and interiorizing its ideas and values. This tradition rests upon a historically mediated set of ideas, for which narrative is an especially suitable means of transmission. David Tracy welcomes this "neo-conservative revival", declaring that it "sees through the emptiness of the present and the poverty of the modern subject" and that, unlike fundamentalism, it deserves "full intellectual respect." Here is a theology of retrieval, of rediscovery, that "knows that a present without past memory and tradition is self-illusory and . . . sees the folly of the Enlightenment's wholesale attack on the very concept of tradition."[64]

Although I personally have certain reservations concerning its historical and theological foundations, which I set out in my 1990 Bampton Lectures at Oxford University,[65] it is clear that postliberalism offers an approach that is especially attractive to Anglicanism, with its long-standing emphasis on the importance of operating within a living tradition with deep roots in history. This new emphasis on conducting theology within a living community, conscious of its historical roots and its distinctiveness from other such traditions and communities, allows Christian theology in general and Anglican theology in particular, to pick up and rediscover its foundational ideas and attitudes. Why? The following chapter takes up the story.

6

The Renewal of Anglican Theology
Returning to Roots

The history of Western culture has been deeply affected by the search for roots. Cultural stability and enrichment have often been seen as inextricably linked. This is perhaps most clearly seen in the case of the Italian Renaissance, rightly regarded as one of the most important and creative periods in Western culture. The art galleries and museums of the world are packed full of exhibits showing the remarkable originality and imagination of the new culture that took hold of northern Italy during the period 1350–1550. By the end of the sixteenth century, virtually all of Western Europe had been infected by this astonishing enthusiasm and vision. But what lay behind the magnificent outburst of energy, of incredible artistic excitement, at the time?

The answer to this question is complex. However, a substantial part of that answer can be stated in two Latin words – *"ad fontes*, back to the original sources."* Italian culture gained a new sense of purpose and dignity by seeing itself as the modern heir and champion of the long-dead culture of classical Rome. The Italian Renaissance became a vehicle for bringing the culture of ancient Rome back to life in the modern period. The imaginations of artists, architects, poets, writers, and theologians were seized by this vision. Imagine being able to allow the glory of the past to

115

interact with the cultural void of fourteenth century Italy! And as the process of recollection began, Italy began to gain a reputation as the center of a new civilization in Europe.

It is no accident that Italy was the birthplace and cradle of the Renaissance. The Italian writers of the period appear to have seen themselves as returning to their cultural roots in the world of classical Rome.[1] A stream, they argued, was purest at its source; why not return to that source, instead of being satisfied with the muddy and stagnant waters of existing medieval culture? The past was seen as a resource, a foundational influence whose greatness demanded that it should be allowed a voice in the present. The Italian Renaissance arose through a decision to allow the historical roots of Italian culture to impose upon the present, to inform it, to stimulate it – and to transform it. The explosion of creativity that resulted is an eloquent and powerful witness to the potential effects of returning to cultural roots and allowing them to impact upon the present.

Western Christianity has been deeply affected by this concern for roots. In differing ways, both the sixteenth-century Reformation and the nineteenth-century Oxford Movement represented a systematic attempt to return to the vision of the New Testament or apostolic church. One of the central insights of both reformers such as Luther and Calvin and Anglo-Catholic writers such as Newman and Liddon, is the realization that the church of today needs to be constantly challenged and nourished by returning to its roots in the apostolic era. This is no historical romanticism, based on the belief that things were better in the past than they now are. Rather, it is the realization that the church needs to be reminded of its reason for being there in the first place, if it is ever to regain its sense of mission and purpose in the world. Just as the Renaissance led to an enrichment of European culture by a return to its sources, so the life and witness of the modern church can be enriched and nourished by a constant return to its sources in the New Testament.

At first sight, this respect for roots might seem to be a recipe for a reactionary mindset, encouraging unoriginality and the

116

stifling of creativity. That danger must be conceded. But there is another side to this story. Commitment to a tradition is not equivalent to an encrusted dogmatism, a denial of the freedom to think or of the importance of creativity.[2] To take tradition seriously is to allow the voices of the past to speak to us before turning, with a renewed and informed mind, to face the issues of the present.[3] Freedom to think without an accompanying commitment to a tradition can lead to little more than an unanchored chaos. The twentieth century has provided us with ample historical examples of what happens when a society breaks free from the restraining force of tradition. Nazi Germany and the Stalinist Soviet Union are excellent illustrations of the unacceptable consequences of a break with tradition. Walter Benjamin's "Theses on the Philosophy of History" reflect his despair at the totalitarianism that results when a civilized society chooses to break with its traditional values.[4] It is very easy to break with one's roots; but, as the cultural history of the Soviet Union in recent years makes clear, it is very difficult to pick up those roots, once broken. David Tracy is one of many recent writers within a more liberal tradition to express concern over "the wasteful and complacent obstruction of the rich resources of the tradition."[5]

To return to one's roots is to appreciate the need for continuity and responsibility. The suggestion that we should totally abandon the religious past in favor of some exciting new development (usually imported directly from California) is to be resisted, in the light of recognition of the need to preserve the past as a check on the excesses of the present. It is perhaps only to be expected that the most bizarre recent religious cults, as well as innovative approaches to Christianity, generally have their origins in California, where a deep sense of rootlessness prevails. In his *Evolution of Human Consciousness*, John H. Crook comments on the rise of the "hippie" movement in California at about the time of the Vietnam War: "It is no accident that the impetus came largely from the immigrant state of California where traditional cultural values are perhaps most fragmented and a need for new roots is most pronounced."[6] Anglicanism, with its strong sense of historical *belonging*, lacks this sense of rootlessness and should thus be resistant to many of the destabilizing developments especially associated with Christian churches in this fragmented and unstable region.

A concern for one's roots is important for continuity and stability, nurturing the conditions under which communities may grow and mature. It encourages wariness, exercising a restraining influence upon innovation. An enduring tradition, firmly located in history and taken seriously by those who claim to be its heirs, ensures caution and continuity within that community. Faithfulness to roots is not inconsistent with addressing contemporary needs and opportunities. Indeed, it provides a resource and foundation for renewal and *aggiornamento* in the face of the issues of today.

The Loss of a Vision

One of the central tasks of theology is to present a church with a vision – a vision that embraces what it once was and what it might one day become and that, by doing so, poses a challenge to the present. What happens when a movement loses its vision? What are the results if a movement, originally defined by an inspirational vision, chooses to forget or repress that foundational motivation? In short: what happens if a church breaks with its historical roots?

This is not, I must stress, a hypothetical question. As the history of Methodism in Canada in particular indicates, many mainline denominations have been prone to such pressures, from within or outside the church, in the last century.[7] In the case of Methodism, this has been linked with the perception that its original Wesleyan foundations are increasingly irrelevant to the modern age. The accuracy of this perception has been the subject of some dispute, with many younger American Methodist theologians arguing for a rediscovery of the Wesleyan roots of the movement as an essential prerequisite for a recovery of spiritual and theological vision. The formation of the United Church in Canada and the Uniting Church in Australia, have been less than happy experiences for Methodists. The merger with Presbyterians has, in each case, led to the formation of churches that seem, to

118

outside observers, to have lost their appeal to their original constituencies and to lack any real attraction for outsiders. As a result, they have become dominated by an older generation, who seem increasingly incapable of relating to the major cultural shifts that are taking place in Western society. One of the most informative case studies to date has examined the development of British Quakerism since 1895.[8] In its earlier phase, Quakerism was a distinctive form of Christianity, that placed an emphasis on the role of the Holy Spirit. George Fox wrote of his mission "to turn people from darkness to the light, that they might receive Jesus Christ." Yet this "receiving of Jesus" was elaborated in terms of "obedience to the light." Various early Quaker writers describe this in different ways: some as an "internal principle," some as "the Spirit," others as "the Light." As William Penn put it, "there are divers ways of speaking they have been led to use by which they declare and express what this principle is."

But the rise of "modern thought forms" in the 1890s saw an erosion of the supernaturalist worldview of an earlier generation of Quakers. The specific links between Christianity and Quakerism were set to one side as the movement came to see itself increasingly as a "mystical" or "spiritual" form of religion. In her 1980 Swarthmore Lecture, Janet Scott brought this understanding of Quakerism to its logical conclusion, breaking its distinctive links with Jesus Christ and grounding its identity in a vague notion of an "Inner Light," that bears a marked resemblance to the foundational liberal idea of "universal religious experience."

> If we believe that the Inner Light is available to everyone, we must see God's self-disclosure in many events and lives and a worldwide possibility of interpreting the ways of God. And this is in fact what happens. God is revealed not only in well known ways, the Exodus, the Exile, through Muhammed, Buddha, Gandhi, Guru Nanak, George Fox, but in countless millions of happenings and people, wherever we have eyes to see.

Scott's approach results in Quakerism seeing itself as one

possibility among many of conceptualizing and articulating a universal human possibility. As a result, Quakerism has ceased to have any distinctive position, becoming, in effect, little more than an isolated group protesting at certain trends in mainline religion. It is no longer clear what Quakerism positively represents. It has lost touch with its roots; having chosen to disregard its original foundational vision, it has found itself unable to replace it with another. Faced with the loss of any distinctive vision, it has begun to lose its way. Unless it can regain its vision, it will eventually lose any reason for existing as an entity in its own right.

This loss of vision can easily arise through a lack of concern for one's heritage. In their recent survey of Baptist thought, especially in the United States, Timothy George and David S. Dockery identify the following sentiment as increasingly prevalent among Baptists: "Baptists are not essentially a doctrinal people. We have no creed but the Bible, which everyone should be left to interpret according to his or her personal predilection. The basic criterion of theology is individual experience . . . Baptist means freedom, freedom to think, believe and preach without constraints."[9] It also, as George and Dockery point out, can easily come to mean "rootless." This "full-blown ideology of indifference" has obvious parallels within many mainline denominations, including Anglicanism, as Wade Clark Roof and William McKinney point out in their ground-breaking study of recent trends.

Roof and McKinney here demonstrate how the shift towards inclusiveness and the need to be seen to be "relevant" to an increasingly secular American culture has led to the steady erosion of distinctiveness of the churches. Those who maintain their commitment to historic Christianity find themselves growing: the Southern Baptists, who are currently planting three new churches per day in the United States, have announced plans to expand this to four per day in the near future. Those that have sought to accommodate themselves to secular cultural trends are in decline. However, this is a trend that need not continue. The experiment with cultural accommodation has been tried. It has failed. Now it is time to learn from our brothers and sisters who have commended distinctiveness. As Roof and McKinney comment:

> A crucial challenge for liberal Protestantism is to recapture some sense of particularity as a community of memory and not merely as a custodian of generalized cultural values. This will require among other things a countering of the secular drift that has had a disproportionate impact on its traditional consituency.[10]

Theology concerns the quest for justifiable particularity. For some, this suggestion will seem arrogant and imperialist. Yet, in fairness, it must be pointed out that such criticisms pre-empt any individuals or bodies from laying claim to any distinctive positions whatsoever, lest they be accused of élitism. To be different is not to be superior, but simply to be different. The liberal trend towards homogenization – "we're all saying the same thing" – eliminates the diversity of life in favour of a dull grey monochrome, where none is allowed to be different. But Christianity *is* distinct. After all, Jesus Christ was not crucified just for reinforcing what everyone already knew. With the end of the Enlightenment, the embargo on distintinctiveness has been lifted. No longer is the claim to be saying something *different* seen as equivalent to being irrational. Jews are special; they have a special story and a different set of values. In the same way, Christians are special; they too have a special story and a different set of values.[11] It is perhaps here that liberalism has most failed the church and contributed to its sense of lack of purpose.

The Public Failure of Liberal Theology

Oxford New Testament scholar Robert Morgan is one of many recent writers to point out that "the best insights of liberal theology . . . do not suffice to nourish a minority church in an aggressively secular society."[12] That sentiment is widely echoed today. It is, however, important to ask why this perception has dawned and what its implications might be for a worldwide church poised on the brink of theological renewal and reconstruction. The point at issue is perhaps best appreciated by considering the relation between Christianity and Western culture.

There can be no doubt that, as liberal writers have insisted, the thought, language, and actions of the Christian churches require constant critical examination from those outside the church.[13] Anglicanism has constantly prided itself on being a *thinking* church. However, liberalism has too often seemed intent on judging the church with reference to prevailing cultural norms. As Stanley Hauerwas and John Howard Yoder point out, this can only promote the support of the dominant or prevailing culture, rather than its radical transformation. With the breakdown of what used to be referred to as the "Judaeo-Christian consensus" in the United States and elsewhere, the church has increasingly found itself in a culture that is antithetical to the Christian world-view.

This major development was not anticipated in H. Richard Niebuhr's *Christ and Culture* (1951), a work that has had a major impact on mainline denominational thinking, including that of Anglicanism, on the relationship between Christianity and its cultural milieu. Niebuhr's book is now seen to be fatally flawed because of its fundamental assumption that the churches can *choose* their relation to the prevailing culture.[14] But increasingly, Western culture has the upper hand and chooses to specify *its* relation to the churches. And, as Lesslie Newbigin has stressed, that public stance is predetermined by a commitment to a "normative pluralism" and, in effect, a "public atheism."[15] Richard John Neuhaus has shown how a "naked public square" has resulted from the systematic and deliberate exclusion of religion from American public life.[16] At no point does Niebuhr consider, or even anticipate the possible emergence of, the paradigm "Culture against Christ." Yet precisely this paradigm is being forced upon the churches in the West.

The difficulty for liberalism in recent years is that its cultural accommodationism, initially seen as a virtue, has now proved to make Christian theology a hostage to the dominant cultural ideology, in a manner that shows alarming parallels with the situation that developed in the German Church crisis of the mid-1930s.[17] The Barmen Declaration (1934) was not so much a protest against Hitler and Nazism (though that it unquestionably was); it also represented a passionate affirmation of the need for Christian faith and theology to avoid entangling themselves in the bonds of a prevailing culture. As Hauerwas and Willimon comment:

> For Barth and for us, Nazi Germany was the supreme test for modern theology. There we experienced the "modern world," which we had so labored to understand and to become credible to, as the world, not only of the Copernican world view, computers and the dynamo, but also of the Nazis. Barth was horrified that his church lacked the theological resources to stand against Hitler. It was the theological liberals, those who had spent their theological careers translating the faith into terms that could be understood by modern people and used in the creation of modern civilization, who were unable to say no. Some, like Emanuel Hirsch, even said yes to Hitler.[18]

Hirsch, like so many other German liberal theologians at the time, was unable to discern the dangers of allowing theology to slide into bondage to the prevailing culture – even when that culture became openly Nazi.

The extent and danger of such a bondage varies substantially within the West: in England, the cultural mood remains surprisingly positive; in North America, there is a considerable tension between appproval of the churches at an individual level and the radical application of the doctrine of the "separation of church and state" at the public level; in Australia, Christianity often has to exist in an intensely hostile cultural environment.[19] The assumption that the concerns of the church and the culture go hand in hand may have been valid in the past; today, though not entirely false, it is no longer to be relied upon. It is this shift within the West toward a more overtly secular public stance that underlies Morgan's timely strictures concerning the limitations of liberal theology in nourishing "a minority church in an aggressively secular society." Anglicanism in the West cannot afford to rely on past traditions or memories of religious faith, when such memories are not even shared by the large immigrant communities that are so prominent a feature of modern Western cities.

Yet there are other reasons for expressing anxieties about the liberal approach to theology. The most obvious concern has been expressed repeatedly by non-western Anglicans. This criticism could be summarized as follows. Liberalism rests upon a series of assumptions, grounded in the particularities of Western culture yet treated as if they are universally true and valid premises. For example, the liberal approach to other religions, such as Islam, reflects the pluralist ideology and settled political toleration that is predominant in much of the West. But how can this be applied to a situation such as Pakistan, in which a predominantly and aggressively Islamic culture believes itself to be correct and appears intent upon making Christians conform to it? There is an urgent need in Anglicanism, as within all mainline churches, to foster the development of local theologies, sensitive and responsive to local situations, rather than encourage the false belief that Western assumptions and values have universal validity.[20]

With this observation, we return to the theme of theological renewal, that has been central to this work. One question remains unanswered: who is to work towards this renewal of both Anglicanism and its foundational and controlling theological vision? The final chapter of this work addresses this issue.

7

Theological Education
and
The Renewal of Anglicanism

Christian theology sets out to allow the church to be true to itself. It aims to enable the church to discover for itself why it is there and what it is meant to be doing. Instead of having that meaning and task imposed upon it by outsiders, the church is being invited to discover what it means to be the church of Jesus Christ in the world. Theology allows the church to embrace, critically yet enthusiastically, its roots in the Christian past and supremely in Jesus Christ. That means rediscovering a vision – a vision of what it means to be the church and all that this entails. The new Anglican emphasis upon the church as the bearer of the good news of Jesus Christ, that is now beginning to permeate every level of the church's self-consciousness, has brought with it the possibility of the renewal of a vision. And such a vision is needed if Anglicanism is to retain a distinctive place in modern Western society.

But who is to nourish and tend that vision? Who are to be the guardians of the Anglican theological heritage, that will undergird and inform our churches as they prepare to face the future? The only realistic answer is "our seminaries." This, I must stress, is

125

not the *only* answer; it is however, the only answer that is likely to *work*, especially in the longer term. There is an urgent need for Anglicanism to rediscover the distinctiveness of theological education and recognize its rightful and privileged place within the ministry and mission of the church. Many senior Anglicans still seem to think of the seminary as a combination of a second-rate university and a medieval guild of apprentices. The time has come to insist, both to our church and to the academy at large, that the seminary provides the most authentic environment in which to study theology.

Theological education is becoming a complex matter. My own responsibilities as a theological educationalist neatly illustrate this complexity and force me to the preceding conclusion. My present work links me to three very different educational institutions: one of the world's oldest and most respected universities; a leading Anglican theological college; and one of the largest North American graduate schools of theology.

As research lecturer in theology at the University of Oxford, I am responsible for teaching certain aspects of academic theology (chiefly late medieval theology, the theology of the Reformation and aspects of modern German-language theology) to Oxford undergraduates and postgraduates, often drawn from faculties other than theology, as well as supervising the doctoral research of students. Theology is here treated as an academic subject, worthy of serious consideration at the highest level of scholarly competence at one of the world's greatest universities. In this context, it tends to be treated with a certain degree of detachment by teacher and student alike. As it happens, most students studying theology at Oxford University, as well as most of those whose task it is to educate them, are practicing Christians. Elsewhere, this is not the case.

My second set of responsibilities is to teach theology to men and women in training for ministry at Wycliffe Hall, Oxford, one of Anglicanism's leading centers of theological education. Although the Hall's students are drawn from throughout the world, most are ordinands of the Church of England preparing for ministry in that church. Here, the agenda is very different. Theology is focused towards pastoral ministry, aiming to equip those who will preach, teach and pastor in future. The students are committed, both to the Christian faith and to their vision of future ministry. It is impossible to avoid noticing the difference between these ministerial students and Oxford University undergraduates; at a purely academic level, they are comparable, in that most Wycliffe Hall students have already obtained degrees, often from Oxford or Cambridge. Yet significant differences show up in two major areas: those of *motivation* and *commitment*.

In terms of their motivation, Wycliffe Hall students see theology as an essential part of their equipping to serve God in his church; undergraduates often see it as simply an academic subject – a very interesting academic subject, admittedly, but one among many such others offered at Oxford University. For ordinands, it is different. Theology gives them a framework within which they will live their future lives as pastors and preachers. Ministerial students want to know what the cash value of theology is, understanding how it relates to matters of ethics, spirituality, and apologetics. It is a practical, as well as an academic subject. In common with most university teachers of theology who have taught these two different categories of students, I sense a real difference in perception as to the relevance and importance of their subject. There is no doubt as to which category is the more exciting, rewarding and demanding to teach.

The second major difference concerns commitment. In teaching Oxford University students, questions of personal faith or commitment are generally regarded as off the agenda. It is not meant to matter whether students or those who teach them are practicing Christians. The important thing is to wrestle with Luther's theology of justification, or Karl Barth's Christology, to mention but two themes of interest. But with ministerial students, the agenda is very different. The personal commitment of both student and teacher becomes of importance. Students are looking for guidance as they think through the great theological issues, sort out their own personal positions and apply theology to matters of ministry. They want to know that they can trust those who teach them. More than that; they want to be assured that those who teach them are committed to a vision of theology as the servant of the church, rather than simply as an academic career option. I have noticed how often the question that ministerial students ask about those who teach them is not primarily "Does this guy know about Barth?" (though such competence is valued), but "Is this guy a good role model for pastoral ministry?."

My third field of teaching responsibilities lies in North America. As research professor of systematic theology at Regent College, Vancouver, my responsibilities are to educate a highly literate, intelligent and motivated Christian laity. Regent College, one of North America's largest graduate schools of theology, has, since its founding twenty years ago, dedicated itself to the vision of lay theological education on a transdenominational basis. The success of the school has been legendary, with a substantial part of its student body being drawn from the increasing Christian presence on the Pacific Rim. The school is, in effect, bilingual (English and Cantonese), and a considerable emphasis is placed on Chinese Christianity, a growing presence both in the highly cosmopolitan city of Vancouver itself and in the Pacific constituency from which it draws to such a significant extent. Although the school is transdenominational, Anglicans are well represented among both faculty and students.

I make no secret of the fact that I regard this work to be one of the most rewarding and stimulating of my calling as a theological educationalist. The education of the laity is something that English Anglicanism in particular neglects severely, often apparently regarding its laity as having no roles other than those of paying and praying for their clergy, who invariably know better than they do.[1] With honorable exceptions, chiefly in London and university cities, there is no real equivalent to the "adult Sunday school," so vibrant a feature of most American Anglican churches, that reflects the greater commitment to educating the laity characteristic of that church.

One of my most heartfelt concerns for Anglican theological

education is that it often focuses so narrowly on the clergy. In East Africa, great emphasis is placed upon the prominent and valued role of lay evangelists and catechists in the ministry of the church. Professionalization, perhaps one of the greatest scourges of modern Western culture, has failed to erode the role of the laity in this dynamic Anglican province. Outsiders often comment on how Western Anglicanism devalues its laity, often on the basis of deeply flawed beliefs concerning the "professional" role of the clergy. Theological education is a case in point. Regent College's emphasis on the vital role of the laity in the church is a healthy corrective to the creeping professionalization that has so isolated the clergy from ordinary Christians in the present century and created the impression that theology is an alienating irrelevance. A heartfelt concern to forge theologically-informed approaches to issues of lay leadership and marketplace spirituality is one from which more traditional Anglican theological education could learn much. Our seminaries could learn from this concern from the laity; it is no accident that the areas of greatest Anglican lay involvement also appear to be the areas of greatest expansion.

The Relevance of Theology

Richard John Neuhaus, surveying the output of one leading North American religious publishing house, remarks: "Most clergy, never mind lay people, have given up reading theology."[2] Why? Two reasons are regularly given:

1. Much modern theology is written in a style and using a vocabulary that is alien to the vast majority of its potential reading public and bears little relation to Scripture, the liturgy, or hymns – the three sources of theology most familiar to ordinary Christians.

2. Much modern theology addresses issues that bear little relation to the concerns of the Christian public and seems to center on issues of purely academic interest.

Let me explore the second point further with reference to the novels of David Lodge, for which I have to confess something of an addiction. Lodge, formerly professor of English at the University of Birmingham, is a distinguished student of postmodern literature. His novel *Small World* is a witty and elegant exploration of the inner inconsistencies of deconstruction. A more recent novel, *Nice Work*, asks us to imagine a collision of worlds – the world of a small business in Birmingham, specializing in the manufacture of machine parts and that of a junior lecturer in the department of English at the fictional University of Rummidge (which bears suspicious resemblances to Birmingham), who is deeply influenced by Jacques Derrida.[3] In a marvellously narrated section, Lodge describes the latter's gradual realization that the vital issues of her life – deconstruction, the arbitrariness of the relation between the signifier and signified – are an utter irrelevance to 99.9 percent of the human race. It is a painful realization, that alters her outlook on the academic world.

It is a sad and simple fact of life that much modern theology is perceived as totally pointless, not just by the general public, but even by educated lay Christians. Its vocabulary and concerns seem to belong to a different planet. Even Basil Mitchell, formerly Nolloth Professor of the philosophy of religion at Oxford University, recorded his belief, based on ample personal observation that "often when given the opportunity to explain Christian doctrine and its implications to a potentially receptive audience, theologians have little definite or distinctive to say."[4] Yet the Reformation, to note but one example of a period in Christian history, offers us a vision of a time when theology was directed toward the issues that concerned the Christian public. As a university teacher of theology at Oxford, I cannot help but notice the reaction of theology students to my lectures on the theology of the Reformation: "We can understand what these people are talking about!" is a typical response from students who have been bewildered by the verbal prolixity (often, it has to be said, masking a conceptual shallowness) of the writings of some recent theologians. "They"re dealing with real questions" is another

130

response, grounded in a growing impatience with a university-based theology that seems bent on pursuing questions of purely academic interest. The low esteem in which American state university departments of religion are generally held, both inside and outside those universities, is ultimately a reflection of their inability to relate to any community of faith.

The growing gap between academic theology and the church has led to much theology focusing on issues that appear to be an utter irrelevance to the life, worship, and mission of the church. Adrian Hastings notes the importance of this point in evaluating the weakness of much Anglican theology of the last generation:

> No church can continue for long without a theology possessing a fair measure of internal coherence, one related organically both to the actual religious practice of believers and to certain basis requirements of credibility or utility posited by contemporary society . . . By the 1970s the central tradition of English academic theology as taught at Oxford and Cambridge, was hardly fulfilling these needs. There had long been a notable gap between academic theology and what one may call a theology of the pew, but in previous ages there had remained a link between them. The theology of Gore, Temple, Ramsey or Farrer was, most certainly, one the church could live and thrive with. The same cannot be said for that of Nineham, Hick or Cupitt . . . It is no refutation of their work to say that there is simply no future for a church that can produce no reasoned expression of its faith stronger than what the dominant theologians of the seventies were able to muster.[5]

This persuasive historical analysis, that has commanded widespread assent in English Anglican circles, clearly gives rise to a vital theological challenge: that Anglicanism should give its attention to a "reasoned expression of its faith" which has both relevance and credibility at the parish level. But who will produce such a theology? If theologians are not themselves engaged in ministry, it is perhaps inevitable that their theology will become introverted, reflecting the interests of an academic community whose standing continues to fall in public estimation.[6]

The issues that are today treated with what often approaches polite contempt by academic theologians were regarded as of vital importance by Christian writers of the past – issues such as the nature of the true church, the proper relation of the church and state, the grounds of Christian assurance and a direct answer to the age-old question, "What must I do to be saved?," that many modern theologians would dismiss as premodern or having no academic significance. Yet these issues are still debated today. Indeed, they continue to be of vital importance to the church, especially in regions of the world in which Christianity is either expanding into new regions or facing hostility or persecution from rival belief systems, especially Islam. The church needs all the help it can get from its thinkers in wrestling with such issues. But these issues are now largely debated *outside* the academy, in local church study groups, in university Bible studies and in seminaries.

The academy has thus become seriously isolated from the heartbeat of Christianity, especially in the United States. Happily, this has happened to a far lesser extent in the United Kingdom; in Australia, there are even moves to bring Christian theology back into tertiary education, after years of enforced isolation. Nevertheless, the danger remains. Theology must learn to address issues that are of real concern to ordinary Christians and to the church at large, on the basis of assumptions and approaches that are recognizably Christian. Otherwise, they will be dismissed – as they deserve to be dismissed – by the church. This anxiety is also reflected in the status of the theologian, to which we now turn.

The Status of the Theologian

One of the greatest privileges is to be party to other people's conversations. While spending four months as a visiting professor of theology at a leading theological seminary of the United Methodist Church in the United States several years ago, I was able to listen to the debate taking place among both faculty members and ministerial students of that church over the issue of commitment on the part of seminary teachers. Perhaps because I was a visitor to the theological school, views were expressed with a frankness that otherwise might not have been forthcoming. Many of the students expressed grave reservations about some of their teachers, chiefly for two reasons.

First, they sensed that many of those teachers saw themselves as academic theologians who had yet to find university appointments and were merely waiting for such a position to open up for them. Their hearts were not in ministerial education; this was simply an inferior option that they had been obliged to select, owing to a lack of a more prestigious position at present. The students noticed the difference in attitude between that type of faculty member and those whose hearts were given to ministerial training. Some of the faculty believed passionately that there was no greater privilege than to teach, train and encourage the pastors of tomorrow. They were teaching in seminaries because they *wanted* to be there and had no intention of going on to the higher status positions in the universities. It seemed to me to be no accident that these were the faculty members held in highest esteem by the students, sensing that their future calling as ministers was valued by those who were responsible for educating them.

As the study of church history suggests, we have been here before. For example, in the Middle Ages, theologians were often equally isolated from the community of faith, closeted within the confines of the monastic life and often writing for an audience of their fellow monks. In more recent times theologians have again become increasingly detached from the communities that they are meant to serve. They have become more and more professionalized, isolated within academic theological faculties and becoming vulnerable to the charge of dwelling within ivory towers. Professionalization has tended to remove theologians from within the communities of faith and has placed them within the narrow confines of the universities, just as that same professionalization has isolated pastors from theology, forcing a gap between theology and the church. Secularization has led to a separation of personal faith and academic life; the professional academic theologian need not have any commitment to the faith or life of the church.

133

THE RENEWAL OF ANGLICANISM

Yet church history offers us alternative approaches. To note but one example, the Reformation bridges the gap between these two unsatisfactory approaches to the function of theology and offers a working model to contemporary Anglicanism. The Reformers, however diverse their origins may have been, were individuals who were based in the cities of Europe, living within the communities that they served and sharing their faith. They were isolated by neither monastery nor university from the people who looked to them for guidance. Their task was to interpret and apply the gospel to the concrete situations in which they found themselves – above all, in relating to the lives of ordinary people.

Perhaps one of the most important moments of the Reformation may be traced to 1520, when Martin Luther made the momentous and dramatic decision to cease being a purely academic reformer, addressing academic issues and audiences and instead to make a direct and passionate appeal to the religious hopes and faith of the German people. Luther became both a preacher and a pastor – and his pastoral concern and experience shows up, time and time again, in his theology. Luther read and interpreted the New Testament as one who believed that it was of vital and continuing relevance to the life of the Christian community. His is a genuine pastoral theology, a theology that addresses the needs and concerns of ordinary believers and those who seek to minister to them. Similarly, throughout Calvin's writings we find a determination to engage with the real world of everyday life in the city of Geneva, along with all the problems and possibilities this brings with it. Calvin wrote, worshiped, and preached as a member of the community that he addressed. He was not apart from its members; he was not above them; rather, he wrote from within his community, as part of it, sharing its life and its problems. His was no theology imposed from above or from outside the church, but a theology generated within a community, with the needs and aspirations of that community in mind.

Is there not a model here that has relevance and appeal for Anglicanism today? Again and again, ordinary Christians today comment on how irrelevant they consider theologians to be. "They seem so distant." "They don't seem to understand the problems of everyday life." "They seem to have a totally different agenda from ordinary believers." "We can't understand what they are going on about." In brief, academics (and academics who become bishops!) often get a very bad popular press. These comments are deeply revealing, indicating the considerable gulf that has opened between the academy and the church and the urgent need to bridge between them. These perceptions of a massive gap between church and academy are too easily reinforced by perusing the abstracts of the American Academy of Religion, where one encounters suggestions, such as the following, that seem to make depressingly little sense as English prose or as Christian theology:

> Taylor's metaphorical "body," then, is an (ex)tension of the phallocentric and phallocratic technology of modern theology, now confined to a two-dimensional wordplay indifferent to the cries and joys of a richly signed wor(l)d.[7]

Quite so. Surely, many ask, must there not be a more satisfactory way of conceiving the task, calling, and responsibilities of the theologian, than that offered by academic theology?

It is thus vitally important to note that the Christian tradition makes available alternative models, with a distinguished history of application – such as the model of the theologian as one who is called to serve the community of faith from within. Part of that service is criticism of its ideas and outlooks, but it is a loving and caring criticism on the basis of shared Christian beliefs and commitments, rather than the modern criticism of the Christian community by academic "theologians" on the basis of secular beliefs and values, often radically agnostic or atheistic, which that community feels no pressing reason to share.

This approach was developed by the Marxist writer Antonio Gramsci (1891–1937),[8] who used the sixteenth-century Reformation as a paradigm for his notion of the "organic intellectual." This idea is of considerable importance to contemporary Anglicanism, as it seeks to redisover the proper place of theology within its ranks. Gramsci argues that two distinct types of intellectuals can be discerned. In the first place, there are those who are imposed upon a community by an external authority. These "traditional intellectuals" were not chosen by that community and have influence only insofar as that authority is imposed upon the community. In contrast to this, Gramsci notes – and commends – the idea of an "organic intellectual," understood as one who arises within a community and who gains authority on account of his or her being seen to represent the outlook of that community. Such persons' authority is not imposed but emerges naturally, reflecting the esteem in which the community holds them and its willingness to regard them as its representative thinkers.

This model of the theologian is enormously helpful. It resonates with the experience of many people within Anglicanism, who have come to regard "professional theologians" with intense scepticism as a result of the irresponsibility of the 1960s and 1970s. Theologians must now earn their spurs within Anglicanism, gradually gaining respect and commanding authority within that community on account of their observable fidelity and commitment to its ethos and norms, their ability to express themselves and their concern for the well-being of the church and its members.[9] John R. W. Stott of the evangelical wing of the church is an excellent example of an "organic intellectual." He possesses no academic or institutional authority worth speaking of, but rightly enjoys enormous status within the world-wide Anglican community (and beyond) on account of his having *earned* that respect. Precisely the same could be said of Richard Holloway of the catholic wing of the church; even before his appointment as bishop of Edinburgh, he was regarded with considerable respect within world-wide Anglicanism. People regarded him as having authority because he had been accepted as being *worthy* of possessing authority. There was an organic and natural relationship between this person and the community for whom he spoke and to whom he so clearly holds himself responsible.

In the past, Anglicanism has been prone to seduction by the reputation of the academy. If one wanted to know what Christians believed on a particular issue, one turned to a professor of theology at some respected university. Surrounded by an aura of academic respectability, this personage was deemed to be the most authoritative source available. But Gramsci encourages us to look instead towards the community of faith, to seek and find authority in individuals with a proven record of fidelity to the Christian tradition, a concern for the *consensus fidelium,* a love for the gospel and a responsible and informed concern to relate it to the world – whether recognized by the academy or not. The best intellectuals may exist and operate outside the academy!

This is not to suggest that being a Christian academic, or a professor of theology at a distinguished university, disqualifies someone from having authority within the community of faith. Nor is it to say that there is any place for anti-intellectualism inside the church. The point is simply that such qualifications are not in themselves adequate grounds for the possession of such authority. The ideal focus of such authority within Anglicanism is, in any case, the bishop rather than the professor.[10] Ideally one would hope that Anglicanism might produce rather more bishops who have such an "organic authority," whereby their consecration confirms what is evidently already present, rather than imposes what is conspicuously absent.

The notion of an "organic intellectual" is also of importance in relation to the authority exercised by a bishop who seeks to impose his or her personal views upon a church, when these do not correspond to the "mere Christianity" (C. S. Lewis) of ordinary believers. Organic authority is something that *emerges,* not something that is *imposed.* And it collapses if the individual in question proves to have lost support within the community, by failing to reflect its beliefs and values. A trend-setting report of the Episcopal Church in the United States, entitled *Theological Freedom and Social Responsibility,* recognized how individuals in a position of *institutional* authority could lose their *organic* authority, putting them in a position in which, having lost the latter, they could no longer meaningfully retain the former:

We do believe that if an individual finds himself unable, in good conscience, to identify with the living tradition of the church, reflected in the Bible, the creeds and, especially for Anglicans, in the liturgy of the Book of Common Prayer, he should as a matter of personal integrity voluntarily remove himself from any position in which he might be taken as an official spokesman for the whole community.[11]

Gramsci's approach allows us to draw a distinction between the institutional or traditional authority exercised by virtue of a church position and the authority that arises from the esteem and trust in which an individual is held. A bishop who exercises authority *de jure* may have lost that authority *de facto*, in that the community may refuse to regard him or her as having any right to speak to them or for them. Such an individual would merely exercise ecclesiastical power without commanding spiritual authority.

Recovering a Vision for Theological Education

In his *Theologia: The Fragmentation and Unity of Theological Education*, Edward Farley points to a series of developments in theological education that have led to the loss of a defining theological vision characterized by the coinherence of piety and intellect. Farley argues that the term *theologia* has lost its original meaning, which he defines – a little lugubriously, one feels – as "sapiential and personal knowledge of divine self-disclosure," that leads to "wisdom or discerning judgment indispensable for human living." Elsewhere, he lapses into plain English and refers to the original vision of theology as "not just objective science, but a personal knowledge of God and the things of God."[12]

Christian theology cannot remain faithful to its subject matter if it regards itself as purely propositional or cognitive in nature. The Christian encounter with God is transformative. As John Calvin pointed out, to know God is to be changed by God; true knowledge of God leads to worship, as the believer is caught up in a transforming and renewing encounter with the living God. To know God is to be changed by God.[13] The idea of a purely "objective" or "disinterested" knowledge of God is thus precluded.

138

For someone to speak objectively about "knowing God" is as realistic as the lover speaking dispassionately of the beloved. As Søren Kierkegaard pointed out in his *Unscientific Postscript*, to know the truth is to be known by the truth. "Truth is something which affects our inner being, as we become involved in an appropriation process of the most passionate inwardness."[14]

Theology, in this classic sense of the term, is a "heartfelt knowledge of divine things" (Farley), something that affects the heart and the mind. It relates to both *fides quae creditur* and *fides qua creditur*, the objective content of faith and the subjective act of trusting. But all this has changed, not on account of any fundamental difficulties with this classic conception of theology, but on account of the increasing professionalization and specialization of theological educators. The study of theology has become little more than the mastery of discrete bodies of data. It has something you just know about – where it should be something that shapes your life, provides a reason to live and gives direction to ministry. It is thus no wonder that so many seminaries report a burgeoning interest in spirituality on the part of their students, when they have been starved of the experiential and reflective dimensions of theology by the unwarranted intrusion of the academic attitude toward this subject. Yet when the Perkins School of Theology (a United Methodist school in Dallas, Texas) introduced spiritual formation as a curriculum requirement, some faculty and students expressed misgivings about the presence of the course within an academic community.[15] The idea of theology as a purely academic subject forces issues of personal spiritual formation and Christian living – originally an intergal part of the idea of "theology" – out on a limb. The time has come to welcome them back and rediscover what theology is meant to be all about.

There is an increasing recognition of the importance of spiritual formation as an aspect of a rounded theological education.[16] The study of theology is recognized to be transformative, in that one is recognized not merely to be wrestling with *texts*; nor yet with *ideas*, but with *the living God*. Theology can so easily become the study of theologians; its proper subject is the study of God.

Yet the term "spirituality" needs to be used with caution. Owen Chadwick, until recently professor of modern history at the University of Cambridge, has pointed out how the origins of the modern term "spirituality" and many other related terms (such as "the inner life" or "the interior life") lie in the French spiritual writings of the seventeenth century.[17] From its beginnings, the term has strong associations with "a striving after the purely immaterial." The word "spirituality" thus appears to have been associated initially with a radical division between the spiritual and the physical, between the soul and the body, between contemplation and everyday life. It implies that its subject is primarily the interior nurture of the soul, undertaken in withdrawal from the distractions of ordinary life. The older vocabulary of the Anglican tradition reflects more faithfully a central aspect of its spirituality – the total integration of faith and everyday life.[18] Anglicanism has a long tradition of "doing theology on the ground." Its greatest writers have tended to be poets (such as George Herbert and John Keble), clerics (such as Richard Hooker), bishops (such as Jeremy Taylor, Michael Ramsey, and William Temple) and laity (such as Dorothy L. Sayers and C. S. Lewis). It is a tradition that needs to be renewed – and the seminaries provide a unique, organic and natural context for this renewal.

This point must be allowed to have a direct bearing on seminary faculty recruitment policies. Some Anglican seminaries still work on the basis of the highly problematic assumption that the best candidates for teaching posts will be those who are the most highly academically qualified. But what of his or her commitment to ministry? What of his or her understanding of the role of theology within the church? My own experience, in England and North America, suggests that some seminaries still regard their faculty as potential university teachers who have yet to find their niche and see their seminary teaching position as an interim half-measure between unemployment and a tenured university appointment. There is a real need for Anglicanism to make its seminary professors feel valued and encourage them in the vision of forging a truly *pastoral* theology, in which the full resources of the Christian tradition are brought to bear on the pastoral and evangelistic tasks of the church.[19]

Anglican theology can be renewed, provided that it is *root- and task-orientated*. In other words, it must be faithful to the Christian tradition on the one hand and must apply itself to the pastoral and evangelistic tasks of the church on the other. We need to rediscover that theology does not mean "the study of theologians" but "the study of *God*." The academy has set a purely academic agenda for too long; it is time to redress that balance.

Anglican theology has always been at its best when it is conscious of its theological roots, its ecclesiastical identity and its pastoral concerns. In his *Republic*, Plato argued that the world would be a better place only when "philosophers were kings and kings philosophers." There is a sense in which the church would benefit considerably if pastors were to be theologians and theologians pastors. Yet precisely this insight is found in classical Anglicanism, before modernity imposed its alienating idea of "professionalization" on the discipline of theology and insisted that theology should be an academically neutral discipline conducted in isolation from the church. That experiment has been unsuccessful. As historians of twentieth-century Anglicanism have pointed out, it has led to the production of a theology that is a pastoral irrelevance and spiritually barren and of late has not even been distinguished by academic excellence.[20]

The academic study of theology has forced an artificial division between theology and spirituality. Karl Barth is rumored to have been in the habit of beginning his lectures with prayer, or even a hymn. This practice would probably be outlawed in North American faculties of religion today. Yet it points to the close link between theology and adoration, a link brought out so clearly by the Methodist writer Geoffrey Wainwright in his deservedly acclaimed work *Doxology*.[21]

The same point has also been made by Anglican writers, both catholic and evangelical. The noted Anglican evangelical theologian James I. Packer is a case in point. In a published lecture entitled "An Introduction to Systematic Spirituality," Packer

141

stressed the utter impossibility of separating theology and spirituality:

> I question the adequacy of conceptualizing the subject-matter of systematic theology as simply revealed truths about God and I challenge the assumption that has usually accompanied this form of statement, that the material, like other scientific data, is best studied in cool and clinical detachment. Detachment from what, you ask? Why, from the relational activity of trusting, loving, worshipping, obeying, serving and glorifying God: the activity that results from realizing that one is actually in God's presence, actually being addressed by him, every time one opens the Bible or reflects on any divine truth whatsoever. This . . . proceeds as if doctrinal study would only be muddled by introducing devotional concerns; it drives a wedge between . . . knowing true notions about God and knowing the true God himself.[22]

Packer's point is that a genuine experience of God makes the detached study of God an impossibility – a point appreciated by medieval mystical writers, who often spoke in rapturous terms of their experience and knowledge of God. It is like asking the lover to be neutral about the beloved. Commitment is not merely a natural outcome of an authentically Christian experience and knowledge of God; it is the substantiating hallmark of such experience and knowledge.

Anglican seminaries, by their very nature, provide an ideal context in which to pursue this vision. Theology is taught in the context of a worshiping and prayerful community, that is aware that to speak of God is potentially to end up adoring and worshiping him and proclaiming him to the world. God is at his most real when he ceases to be an object of inquiry and becomes one who addresses us as his beloved, beckoning to us and inviting us to discover him in his fulness. The study of Christian theology in a committed liberal context, such as that found in most North American state university faculties of religion, must therefore be regarded as inauthentic, imposing totally artificial limitations upon what the "knowledge of God" might be like and what its consequences should be. The systematic exclusion, as a matter of public polity, of prayer and adoration from such teaching results in a truncated and deficient understanding of theology. Seminaries have a unique opportunity to "let God be God" and respond to him accordingly. They need to regain a sense of their distinctiveness at this point and to get rid of the outmoded and unjustified belief that they are somehow second-rate contexts for the learning of theology. The seminary provides a unique environment in which theology is taught by the committed to the committed, in a nourishing atmosphere of prayer, adoration, and pastoral care, with a view to going out into the world convinced that the church has something *distinctive* to say and do.

The seminaries have a vital role to play in the future of Anglicanism – not by mimicking the values and attitudes of secular academia, but by fostering a quiet confidence in the intellectual, spiritual, and moral relevance of the Christian faith to communities and individuals in the modern world.[23] They must regain a sense of calling and of distinctiveness, appreciating that they provide an environment in which the cognitive, experiential, and personal elements of faith can be nourished, stimulated and sustained. It is worth recalling, in this context, that many of the greatest theologians to have served the Roman Catholic church in the present century, such as Yves Congar and Hans Urs von Balthasar, never held university appointments. Academic excellence implies neither an exclusively academic context nor pastoral irrelevance. An Anglican seminary, by recollecting its foundational vision of its purpose, can recreate the best possible environment in which to study and be shaped by Christian theology.

Conclusion

Anglicanism may stand on the brink of a renewal – a renewal that it can and must embrace by reclaiming a vision of what it means to be Christian, returning to our Christian roots and rediscovering why the church came into being in the first place. It means recovering a sense of excitement and exhilaration over the gospel, as we seek to understand how attractive it can be for ourselves before proclaiming its attraction to others. It means regaining confidence in the Christian message in the modern world. It means appreciating the stabilizing influence of the long Anglican tradition and the sense of "belonging in history" that it brings us.

It also means realizing that Western Anglicanism now operates in a missionary rather than a settled pastoral context. Some see this as a depressing situation, reflecting a demoralizingly severe erosion of faith within its former heartlands. Others see it as a moment of challenge and opportunity, when the church can once more become the bearer of the glad tidings of all that God has done and will do for his world. By addressing this missionary situation, the church can once more rediscover its unique and God-given identity and purpose. The history of the Christian church suggests that it is in periods of complacency – such as in the late Middle Ages, or in eighteenth-century England – that it loses its way. Christianity will survive only if it is inherently worthy of surviving – and that means addressing directly the question of what the church has to say to and offer the world. The Decade of Evangelism offers precisely that focus, forcing the church to answer those questions for itself before it turns to address the world. It is an opportunity for both reflection and renewal, as we prepare to enter the third millennium since the birth of Jesus Christ.

The Decade of Evangelism provides Western Anglicanism with an opportunity to renew its people, its seminaries, its theology and its mission in the world. It remains to be seen whether it will do so. If it does not, Western Anglicanism will become an insignificant element of a dynamic church that is focused on southern Africa and the Pacific Basin. Others will take our place in the West. It is no part of the "essence of Anglicanism" thus to dwindle into insignificance. In the recent past, Anglicanism has gained a reputation for its coolness and detachment. Perhaps the time has come to rediscover the excitement and joy of the gospel and allow this to filter down to our worship, praise and prayer. We hold the key to our own future, which awaits our decision.

Notes

Introduction

1. The papers were published in R. Morgan (ed.), *The Religion of the Incarnation: Anglican Essays in Commemoration of Lux Mundi* (Bristol: Bristol Classical Press, 1989).

2. Ninian Smart, *The Science of Religion and the Sociology of Knowledge* (Princeton: Princeton University Press, 1973), pp. 6–7.

3. Cited in A. M. Ramsey, *The Christian Priest Today* (London: SPCK, 1972), p. 21.

4. See especially Owen Chadwick, *The Secularization of the European Mind in the Nineteenth Century* (Cambridge: Cambridge University Press, 1975). Also of interest are Steve Bruce (ed.), *Religion and Modernization: Sociologists and Historians Debate the Secularization Thesis* (Oxford: Clarendon Press, 1992); Eileen Barker, James A. Beckford and Karel Dobbelaere (eds.), *Secularization, Rationalism and Sectarianism* (Oxford: Clarendon Press, 1993).

5. Matthew Arnold, *Poetry and Prose* (London: Hart-Davis, 1954), pp. 144–45. This image is hinted at by Nicholas Lash in his inaugural lecture (1978) as Norris–Hulse Professor of Divinity at the University of Cambridge: see Nicholas Lash, *Theology on Dover Beach* (London: Darton, Longman and Todd, 1979), pp. 3–23.

6. See, for example, its impact upon George Tyrrell, noted by Nicholas Sagovsky, *Between Two Worlds: George Tyrrell's Relationship to the Thought of Matthew Arnold* (Cambridge: Cambridge University Press, 1983), pp. 142–43.

7. Yet in a letter of 1882, Arnold writes of the "provincial unconsciousness of the English": G. W. E. Russell (ed.), *Letters of Matthew Arnold 1848–88* vol 2 (London: Macmillan, 1895), p. 201.

8. See Judith Herrin, *The Formation of Christendom* (Princeton: Princeton University Press, 1987).

9. Peter and Sue Kaldor, *Where the River Flows: Sharing the*

145

THE RENEWAL OF ANGLICANISM

Gospel in Contemporary Australia (Anzea Publishers: Homebush West, N.S.W., 1988), p. xvii.

10. Thomas C. Oden, *Pastoral Theology* (San Francisco: Harper & Row, 1986), pp. 7–8.

Chapter 1

1. See W. P. Haugaard, *Elizabeth and the Settlement of Religion* (Cambridge: Cambridge University Press, 1968); N. L. Jones, *Faith by Statute: Parliament and the Settlement of Religion* (London: Royal Historical Society, 1982).

2. For an excellent analysis of the development of Anglican understandings of the church, see Paul Avis, *Anglicanism and the Christian Church* (Edinburgh: T. & T. Clark, 1989).

3. William Temple, in *The Lambeth Conference 1930: Encyclical Letter from the Bishops* (London: SPCK, n.d.), pp. 113–14.

4. An excellent example is provided by S. Sykes and J. Booty (eds.), *The Study of Anglicanism* (Philadelphia: Fortress Press, 1988).

5. See Alister E. McGrath, "Religion," in J. W. Yolton (ed.), *The Blackwell Companion to the Enlightenment* (Oxford/Cambridge, Mass.: Blackwell, 1992), pp. 447–52.

6. Details in Alister E. McGrath, *The Making of Modern German Christology* (Oxford/Cambridge, Mass.: Blackwell, 1986); Stephen Neill and Tom Wright, *The Interpretation of the New Testament, 1861–1986* new ed. (Oxford: Oxford University Press, 1988).

7. For an accessible introduction, see N. T. Wright, *Who Was Jesus?* (Grand Rapids: Eerdmans, 1993), pp. 1–18.

8. Leslie Houlden, in J. Hick (ed.), *The Myth of God Incarnate* (London: SCM Press, 1977), p. 125.

9. On these general themes, see Diogenes Allen, *Christian Belief in a Postmodern World* (Louisville: Westminster/John Knox Press, 1989); Thomas C. Oden, *After Modernity . . . What? Agenda*

146

Notes

for Theology (Grand Rapids: Zondervan, 1990).

10. Details may be found in Matei Calinescu, *Five Faces of Modernity* (Durham: Duke University Press, 1987); Terry Eagleton, *The Ideology of the Aesthetic* (Oxford: Blackwell, 1990); Kevin Hart, *The Trespass of the Sign* (Cambridge: Cambridge University Press, 1989); David Harvey, *The Condition of Postmodernity* (Oxford: Blackwell, 1989); Christopher Norris, *What's Wrong with Postmodernism?* (Baltimore: John Hopkins Press, 1990).

11. For the suppression of the narrative character of Scripture in response to the pressures of the Enlightenment, see Hans Frei, *The Eclipse of Biblical Narrative: A Study in Eighteenth and Nineteenth Century Biblical Hermeneutics* (New Haven/London: Yale University Press, 1977). For the new interest in narrative theology, see Ronald F. Thiemann, *Revelation and Theology: The Gospel as Narrated Promise* (Notre Dame: University of Notre Dame, 1985); Garrett Green, *Scriptural Authority and Narrative Interpretation* (Philadelphia: Fortress Press, 1987).

12. Louis Weil, "The Gospel in Anglicanism," in S. Sykes and J. Booty (eds.), *The Study of Anglicanism* (Philadelphia: Fortress Press, 1988), pp. 51–76; quote at p. 75.

13. Laurel Clyde, *In A Strange Land: A History of the Anglican Diocese of Riverina* (Melbourne: Hawthorn Press, 1979).

14. See Stephen Judd and Kenneth Cable, *Sydney Anglicans: A History of the Diocese* (Sydney: Anglican Information Office, 1987).

15. Jürgen Moltmann, "An Open Letter to José Miguez Bonino," *Christianity and Crisis* (29 March, 1976): 57–63; quote at p. 60.

16. E. Bolaji Idowu, *Towards an Indigenous Church* (Oxford: Oxford University Press, 1965), p. 5.

17. See P. Chenchiah, *Rethinking Christianity in India* (Madras: Sudarisanam, 1938); Charles Nyamiti, *African Theology: Its Problems, Nature and Methods* (Kampala: Gaba Institute, 1971).

18. Robert J. Schreiter, *Constructing Local Theologies* (Maryknoll, N.Y.: Orbis, 1986), p. 11.

19. Kwame Bediako, "The Roots of African Theology,"

International Bulletin of Missionary Research 13/2 (1989): 58–65. The point is developed at much greater depth in his 1983 Ph.D. thesis (University of Aberdeen), entitled "Identity and Integration: An Inquiry into the Nature and Problems of Indigenization in Selected Early Hellenistic and Modern African Christian Writers."

20. See John H. Mbiti, *Bible and Theology in African Christianity* (Nairobi, Kenya: Oxford University Press, 1986). There is also some fascinating material to be found in the earlier study of David B. Barrett, *Schism and Renewal in Africa* (London: Oxford University Press, 1968).

21. T. E. Yates, "Anglicans and Mission," in S. Sykes and J. Booty (eds.), *The Study of Anglicanism* (Philadelphia: Fortress Press, 1988), pp. 429–41; quote at p. 441.

22. *The Truth Shall Make You Free: The Lambeth Conference 1988* (London: Anglican Consultative Council, 1988), Resolution 43, p. 231.

23. See Vinay Samuel and Christopher Sugden, *Lambeth: A View from the Two Thirds World* (London: SPCK, 1989), pp. 50–75.

24. *The Truth Shall Make You Free*, Resolution 44, p. 231.

25. *The Truth Shall Make You Free*, p. 32.

26. For the notion, see Anthony Brewer, *Marxist Theories of Imperialism: A Critical Survey* (London: Routledge & Kegan Paul, 1980). Lenin's pamphlet can be found reprinted in vol. 22 of *Collected Works*. 45 vols. (Moscow: Progress Publishers, 1960–70).

27. Karl Rahner, cited *International Bulletin of Missionary Research* 11/1 (1987): 11.

28. Stephen Sykes, "An Anglican Theology of Evangelism," *Theology* 94 (1991): 405–14. I assume that Sykes is here referring to Western Anglicanism; his comments would certainly not apply, for example, to Anglican churches in East Africa.

29. See David Martin, *Tongues of Fire: The Explosion of Protestantism in Latin America* (Oxford: Blackwell, 1990); David Stoll, *Is Latin America Turning Protestant? The Politics of Evangelical Growth* (Berkeley: University of California Press, 1991).

30. For a recent symposium on this theme, see R. T. France and A. E. McGrath (eds.), *Anglican Evangelicals: Their Role and Influence in the Church Today* (London: SPCK, 1993).

31. See Geoffrey Rowell, *The Vision Glorious: Themes and Personalities of the Catholic Revival in Anglicanism* (Oxford: Oxford University Press, 1983). For further reflections on such themes, see G. Rowell (ed.), *Tradition Renewed: The Oxford Movement Conference Papers* (London: Darton, Longman and Todd, 1986).

32. W. Norman Pittenger, *The Episcopalian Way of Life* (Englewood Cliffs, N.J.: Prentice-Hall, 1957), p. 13.

33. Admittedly, that tradition is becoming fractured here and there, with some bishops, less appreciative of the Anglican ethos than one would like, threatening to alienate those who wish to pursue more traditional approaches to Christianity, not least by dismissing them – and virtually the entire Christian tradition prior to 1800 – as "fundamentalist." If "there are to be no outcasts," evangelicals and catholics must be welcomed and allowed to function fully within the church. Nevertheless, the tradition generally remains intact.

34. Timothy George, *The Future for Theological Education Among Southern Baptists* (Birmingham, Ala.: Beeson Divinity School, 1989), p. 11 (no pagination in original).

35. John Finney, *Finding Faith Today: How Does it Happen?* (Swindon: Bible Society, 1992). A study guide to this survey, especially useful for church study groups, is also available: John Young, *Journey into Faith* (Swindon: Bible Society, 1992).

36. John Waterhouse, "The Crisis of Evangelicalism," *On Being* 19/3 (1992): 4–8; quote at p. 7.

37. For a comparison of evangelical ecclesiologies, see Robert C. Walton, "A Mixed Body or a Gathered Church of Visible Saints: John Calvin and William Ames," in W. van't Spijken (ed.), *Calvin: Erbe und Auftrag* (Kampen: Kok Pharos, 1991), pp. 168–78.

Chapter 2

1. Adrian Hastings, *A History of English Christianity 1920–1985* (London: Collins, 1986), pp. 532–60.

2. Leslie Paul, *The Deployment and Training of the Clergy* (London: Church Information Office, 1964).

3. See Wade Clark Roof and William McKinney, *American Mainline Religion: Its Changing Shape and Future* (New Brunswick, N.J.: Rutgers University Press, 1987).

4. Ian Breward, *Australia: The Most Godless Place Under Heaven?* (Melbourne: Beacon Hill Books, 1988), pp. 59–78; Bruce Wilson, *Can God Survive in Australia?* (Sydney: Albatross Books, 1983), pp. 11–27.

5. See his *Taking Leave of God* (London: SCM Press, 1980).

6. Hastings, *History of English Christianity*, p. 545. The most important scholarly protest against this trend was Eric L. Mascall, *Theology and the Gospel of Christ: An Essay in Reorientation* (London: SPCK, 1977).

7. Ted Peters, *The Cosmic Self: A Penetrating Look at Today's New Age Movement* (San Francisco: HarperCollins, 1991).

8. Wolfhart Pannenberg, "Religious Pluralism and Conflicting Truth Claims," in G. D'Costa (ed.), *Christian Uniqueness Reconsidered* (Maryknoll, N.Y.: Orbis, 1990), pp. 96–106, quote at p. 100.

9. For an account, see Alister E. McGrath, *The Making of Modern German Christology* (Oxford/Cambridge, Mass.: Blackwell, 1986).

10. Hastings, *History of English Christianity*, pp. 650–51.

11. William Montgomery Brown, *Communism and Christianity* (Gallion, Ohio: Bradford-Brown, 1922), p. 3.

12. John Shelby Spong, *Rescuing the Bible from Fundamentalism* (San Francisco: HarperCollins, 1991).

13. Spong, *Rescuing the Bible from Fundamentalism*, pp. 108–25.

14. John Shelby Spong, *Born of a Woman: A Bishop Rethinks the Birth of Jesus* (San Francisco: HarperCollins, 1992).

15. N. T. Wright, *Who Was Jesus?* (Eerdmans, 1993), pp. 65–92. Wright himself is in the process of writing a major five-volume study of the historical and theological questions surrounding the origins of Christianity, of which the first has now appeared: *The New Testament and the People of God* (London: SPCK, 1992). This work will be of fundamental importance to an informed and reponsible understanding of the issues treated so superficially by Spong.

16. Wright, *Who Was Jesus?*, pp. 91–92.

17. Wright, *Who Was Jesus?*, p. 90.

18. Willow Creek Community Church in South Barrington, Illinois, fills its 4,550-seat auditorium twice on Saturday nights and twice on Sunday mornings by eliminating all matter which is judged to be potentially alienating to the non-religious (such as altars, vestments, hymn books and pipe organs), yet preaching a traditional gospel. Where liberalism introduces cultural accommodation into the gospel proclamation, the approach pioneered at Willow Creek introduces it into the context in which the gospel is preached, eliminating religious trappings where liberalism eliminated religious ideas. Details in Russell Chandler, *Racing Towards 2000: The Forces Shaping America's Religious Future* (San Francisco: HarperSanFrancisco, 1992), pp. 246–55.

19. Spong, *Rescuing the Bible from Fundamentalism*, pp. 35–36.

20. Hugh Mackay, *Reinventing Australia: The Mind and Mood of Australia in the 90s* (Pymble, N.S.W.: Angus & Robertson, 1993).

21. Mackay, *Reinventing Australia*, pp. 21–190.

22. Mackay, *Reinventing Australia*, pp. 234–35.

23. Mackay, *Reinventing Australia*, p. 237.

24. Mackay, *Reinventing Australia*, pp. 243–48.

25. Mackay, *Reinventing Australia*, pp. 238–42.

26. Stanley Hauerwas and William H. Willimon, *Resident Aliens: Life in the Christian Colony* (Nashville: Abingdon Press, 1989), p. 67.

Chapter 3

1. *The Truth Shall Make You Free: The Lambeth Conference 1988* (London: ACC, 1988), p. 32.

2. For background, see Marshall Frady, *Billy Graham: A Parable of American Righteousness* (Boston: Little Brown, 1979); William G. McLoughlin, *Billy Graham: Revivalist in a Secular Age* (New York: Ronald Press, 1960).

3. See John C. Bennett, "Billy Graham at Union," *Union Seminary Quarterly Review* 9 (May 1954): 9–14.

4. *Christianity and Crisis* 16 (March 5, 1956): 18. On Niebuhr, see Richard Wightman Fox, *Reinhold Niebuhr: A Biography* (New York: Pantheon, 1985).

5. *Christianity and Crisis* 16 (April 2, 1956): 40.

6. *Christian Century* 73 (1956): 848–49. This response was provoked by an earlier article by Niebuhr in the same journal: *Christian Century* 73 (1956): 640–42.

7. *Redemptoris Missio: Encyclical Letter of the Supreme Pontiff John Paul II on the Permanent Validity of the Church's Missionary Mandate* (London: Catholic Truth Society, 1991), par. 44.

8. *The Truth Shall Make You Free*, p. 33.

9. *The Truth Shall Make You Free*, p. 32.

10. Richard Hooker, "A Learned Discourse of Justification," vol. 3, *Works* 3d ed. (Oxford: Oxford University Press, 1845), p. 530.

11. *The Truth Shall Make You Free*, p. 32.

12. A. C. A. Hall, *The Doctrine of the Church* (Sewanee, Tenn.: University of the South Press, 1909), pp. 19–20.

13. Alan Richardson, *Christian Apologetics* (London: SCM Press, 1947).

14. See Catherine McGehee Kenney, *The Remarkable Case of Dorothy L. Sayers* (Kent, Ohio: Kent State University Press, 1990); Basil Mitchell, "Contemporary Challenges to Christian Apologetics," *How to Play Theological Ping–Pong* (London: Hodder & Stoughton, 1990), pp. 25–41.

15. John Polkinghorne, *The Way the World Is* (London: SPCK, 1983); *One World* (London: SPCK, 1986); *Science and Creation* (London: SPCK, 1988); *Science and Providence* (London: SPCK, 1989). His earlier book *The Quantum World* (London: Longman, 1984) provides an excellent illustration of his gift of lucid explanation, that finds full expression in his apologetic works.

16. See especially his Barclay Lectures: Hugh Montefiore, *Communicating the Gospel in a Scientific Age* (Edinburgh: Saint Andrew Press, 1988).

17. Richard Holloway, "Evangelicalism: An Outsider's Perspective," in R. T. France and A. E. McGrath (eds.), *Evangelical Anglicans* (London: SPCK, 1993), p. 175.

18. Material here is taken from the *Los Angeles Times*, 12 December 1989, B 1.

19. Donald E. Miller, "Bucking a Powerful Trend," in *All Saints Church Every Member Canvas '90* (Pasadena, 1990). See also his paper "Liberal Church Growth: A Case Study," delivered at the Society for the Scientific Study of Religion, Salt Lake City, Utah, 27–29 October 1989.

20. See J. R. H. Moorman, *The Anglican Spiritual Tradition* (London: Darton, Longman and Todd, 1983); C. J. Stranks, *Anglican Devotion: Studies in the Spiritual Life of the Church of England Between the Reformation and Oxford Movement* (London: SCM Press, 1961); H. R. McAdoo, *Anglican Heritage: Theology and Spirituality* (Norwich: Canterbury Press, 1991).

21. See especially his *Crossfire: Faith and Doubt in an Age of Certainty* (London: Collins, 1990); *The Way of the Cross* (London: Collins, 1986); and more recently his *Another Country, Another King* (London: Collins, 1990), which masterfully mingles spirituality and apologetics.

22. *The Truth Shall Make You Free*, p. 128.

23. *The Truth Shall Make You Free*, p. 31.

24. *Redemptoris Missio*, par. 44. I have altered the translation at one point to allow for inclusive language.

25. A lucid summary of the discussion may be found in Stephen Sykes, "The Fundamentals of Christianity," in S. Sykes and J.

Booty (eds.), *The Study of Anglicanism* (Philadelphia: Fortress Press, 1988), pp. 231–45.

26. I explore this point in my 1990 Bampton Lectures: see *The Genesis of Doctrine* (Oxford/Cambridge, Mass.: Blackwell, 1990), pp. 1–8.

27. *Anglican Consultative Council 1976: Trinidad* (London: ACC, 1976), p. 17.

28. *The Truth Shall Make You Free*, p. 143.

29. *The Truth Shall Make You Free*, p. 32.

30. *Theological Training: A Way Ahead. A Report to the House of Bishops of the Church of England on Theological Colleges and Courses* (London: Church House Publishing, 1992), p. 130.

Chapter 4

1. See John Macquarrie, "The Anglican Theological Tradition," in *Theology, Church and Ministry* (London: SCM Press, 1986), pp. 91–104.

2. See F. Borsch (ed.), *Anglicanism and the Bible* (Wilton, Conn.: Morehouse, 1984). The collection of essays gathered together in R. Bauckham and B. Drewery (eds.), *Scripture, Tradition and Reason: A Study in the Criteria of Christian Doctrine* (Edinburgh: T. & T. Clark, 1988) repays careful study.

3. In general, see Alister E. McGrath, *The Intellectual Origins of the European Reformation* (Oxford/Cambridge, Mass.: Blackwell, 1987), pp. 122–90; see especially pp. 175–90.

4. Peter Fraenkel, *Testimonia Patrum: The Function of the Patristic Argument in the Theology of Philip Melanchthon* (Geneva: Droz, 1961), pp. 13–252.

5. For a full analysis, see Bernhard Lohse, *Ratio und Fides: Eine Untersuchung über die Ratio in der Theologie Luthers* (Göttingen: Vandenhoeck & Ruprecht, 1957). The Latin citation from Luther serves as a motto for this monograph.

6. The best study of this development is John Platt, *Reformed Thought and Scholasticism: The Arguments for the Existence of*

God in Dutch Theology (Leiden: Brill, 1982). On Beza, see Walter Kickel, *Vernunft und Offenbarung bei Theodore Beza* (Neukirchen-Vluyn: Neukirchener Verlag, 1967).

7. The "reason" in question is, of course, Aristotelian: see Denis R. Janz, *Luther on Thomas Aquinas* (Stuttgart: Steiner Verlag, 1989), pp. 17–24. Janz also notes that Luther has few criticisms to make of Aquinas in relation to his use of Scripture; pp. 25–31.

8. See Per Erik Persson, *Sacra Doctrina: Reason and Revelation in Aquinas* (Oxford: Blackwell, 1970).

9. Scotus, *Ordinatio*, preface. See E. Buytaert, "Circa doctrinam Duns Scoti de traditione et de scriptura adnotationes," *Antonianum* 40 (1965): 346–62.

10. See Hermann Schüssler, *Der Primät der Heiligen Schrift als theologisches und kanonistisches Problem im Spätmittelalter* (Stuttgart: Steiner Verlag, 1977).

11. George Lindbeck, *The Nature of Doctrine* (Philadelphia: Fortress Press, 1984). See further Alister E. McGrath, *The Genesis of Doctrine* (Oxford/Cambridge, Mass.: Blackwell, 1990), pp. 20–6.

12. The end result can be seen in my *Iustitia Dei: A History of the Christian Doctrine of Justification* vol. 2 (Cambridge: Cambridge University Press, 1986), pp. 98–111.

13. For a useful analysis, see Michael Oakeshott, *Experience and Its Modes* (Cambridge: Cambridge University Press, 1933). The best general study, from a philosophical standpoint, is Wayne Proudfoot, *Religious Experience* (Berkeley: University of California Press, 1985). For a more theological approach, see Nicholas Lash, *Easter in Ordinary: Reflections on Human Experience and the Knowledge of God* (London: SCM Press, 1988).

14. See Gerhard Ebeling, "Die Klage über das Erfahrungsdefizit in der Theologie als Frage nach ihrer Sache," *Wort und Glaube III* (Tübingen: Mohr, 1975), pp. 3–28.

15. For a useful study, see C. Stephen Evans, *Subjectivity and Religious Belief* (Grand Rapids: Christian University Press, 1976).

16. Lindbeck, *The Nature of Doctrine*. For an assessment and critique, see McGrath, *The Genesis of Doctrine*, pp. 14–34.

17. Stanley Hauerwas, *The Peacaeble Kingdom* (Notre Dame: University of Notre Dame Press, 1983), p. xxi.

18. See Hans-Georg Gadamer, *Truth and Method* (London: Sheed & Ward, 1979), pp. 58–61.

19. See Alister E. McGrath, *Intellectuals Don't Need God and Other Modern Myths: Building Bridges to Faith Through Apologetics* (Grand Rapids: Zondervan, 1993), pp. 30–47.

20. At a popular level, see Alister McGrath and Michael Green, *Springboard for Faith* (London: Hodder & Stoughton, 1993). An expanded version of this book will be published in North America: *Faith has Its Reasons* (Atlanta, Ga.: Nelson, forthcoming).

20. Søren Kierkegaard, *Unscientific Postscript* (London: Oxford University Press, 1941), pp. 169–224. Cf. P. L. Holmer, "Kierkegaard and Religious Propositions," *Journal of Religion* 35 (1955): 135–46.

21. The best-known work to develop his ideas is Jürgen Moltmann's *The Crucified God* (Philadelphia: Westminster Press, 1974). Even the title of this book is a direct quotation from Luther.

22. For a full discussion of Luther's "theology of the cross" see Alister E. McGrath, *Luther's Theology of the Cross* (Oxford/Cambridge, Mass.: Blackwell, 1985).

23. Plato, *Gorgias*, 493b–d.

24. Diogenes Allen, *The Traces of God* (Cambridge, Mass.: Cowley Publications, 1981), p. 19.

25. Augustine, *Confessions*, I.i.1. The quotation is taken from the superb recent translation by Henry Chadwick (Oxford: Oxford University Press, 1991), p. 3.

26. C. S. Lewis, *Surprised by Joy* (London: Collins, 1959), p. 20.

27. C. S. Lewis, "The Weight of Glory," in *Screwtape Proposes a Toast* (London: Collins, 1965), pp. 97–98.

28. Simone Weil, *Waiting for God* (New York: Putnam, 1951), p. 210.

29. Lewis, "The Weight of Glory," p. 99.

30. For what follows, see McGrath, *Luther's Theology of the Cross*. For the implications of this approach for Christian

spirituality, see Alister McGrath, *Roots that Refresh: A Celebration of Reformation Spirituality* (Grand Rapids: Zondervan, forthcoming).

31. Lewis, *Surprised by Joy*, p. 20.

32. C. S. Lewis, "The Language of Religion," in *Christian Reflections* (London: Collins, 1981), p. 169.

33. See further McGrath, *Genesis of Doctrine*, pp. 72–80.

34. For its importance in modern pastoral theology, see Thomas C. Oden, *Pastoral Theology* (San Francisco: Harper & Row, 1986), pp. 3–18.

Chapter 5

1. John Henry Newman is the most celebrated proponent of the idea. See H. D. Weidner, *The "Via Media" of the Anglican Church by John Henry Newman* (Oxford: Clarendon Press, 1990).

2. See W. P. Haugaard, *Elizabeth and the Settlement of Religion* (Cambridge: Cambridge University Press, 1968); N. L. Jones, *Faith by Statute: Parliament and the Settlement of Religion* (London: Royal Historical Society, 1982).

3. See the outstanding study of Martin Heckel, "Reichsrecht und 'Zweite Reformation': Theologisch-juristische Probleme der reformierten Konfessionalisierung," in Heinz Schilling (ed.), *Die reformierte Konfessionalisierung in Deutschland – Das Problem der "Zweiten Reformation"* (Gütersloh: Gerd Mohn, 1986), pp. 11–43.

4. R. Morgan (ed.), *The Religion of the Incarnation: Anglican Essays in Commemoration of Lux Mundi* (Bristol: Bristol Classical Press, 1989), p. xvi. The point is further discussed in Alister E. McGrath, "Dogma und Gemeinde: Zur sozialen Funktion des christlichen Dogmas," *Kerygma und Dogma* 37 (1991): 24–43.

5. For an excellent discussion, see Oliver O'Donovan, *On the Thirty-Nine Articles: A Conversation with Tudor Christianity* (Exeter: Paternoster Press, 1986).

6. On this, see Stephen Neill, *The Spirit of Anglicanism* 3d ed. (Harmondsworth: Penguin Books, 1965); H. R. McAdoo, *The Spirit*

of Anglicanism (London: A & C Black, 1965).

7. See Alister E. McGrath, *The Intellectual Origins of the European Reformation* (Oxford: Blackwell, 1987), pp. 140–51.

8. See Peter Fraenkel, *Testimonia Patrum: The Function of the Patristic Argument in the Theology of Philip Melanchthon* (Geneva: Droz, 1961), pp. 13–252.

9. This focus on both the New Testament and the patristic period has also given rise to one of the most distinctive aspects of Anglicanism in recent times – its emphasis on New Testament and patristic scholarship. It is fair to point out that most of Anglicanism's greatest theologians are, in fact, patristic scholars, Henry Chadwick and Maurice F. Wiles being excellent examples.

10. Richard Hooker, *Laws of Ecclesiastical Polity* vol. 1, in *Works*, 3d ed. (Oxford: Oxford University Press, 1845), p. 339.

11. See the Episcopalian report *Theological Freedom and Social Responsibility* (New York: Seabury Press, 1967), p. 8. See also the Church of England reports *Christian Believing* (London: SPCK, 1976) and *Believing in the Church: The Corporate Nature of Faith* (London: SPCK, 1981).

12. *The Fundamentals: A Testimony of the Truth.* 12 vols. (Chicago: Testimony Publishing Company, 1910–15).

13. The definitive study remains George Marsden, *Fundamentalism and American Culture: The Shaping of Twentieth Century Evangelicalism 1870–1925* (New York: Oxford University Press, 1980).

14. James Davison Hunter, "Fundamentalism in Its Global Contours," in N. J. Cohen (ed.), *The Fundamentalist Phenomenon* (Grand Rapids: Eerdmans, 1990), pp. 56–72; quote at p. 57 (emphasis in original).

15. Nancy Ammerman, *Bible Believers: Fundamentalists in the Modern World* (New Brunswick, N.J.: Rutgers University Press, 1987).

16. Martin E. Marty, "Fundamentalism as a Social Phenomenon," in George Marsden (ed.), *Evangelicalism and Modern America* (Grand Rapids: Eerdmans, 1984), pp. 56–70.

17. See Claus-Peter Clasen, *Anabaptism: A Social History,*

1525–1618 (Ithaca and London: Cornell University Press, 1972) and especially G. H. Williams, *The Radical Reformation* 3d ed. (Kirksville, Miss.: Sixteenth Century Journal Publishers, 1992).

18. Bradley J. Longfield, *The Presbyterian Controversy: Fundamentalists, Modernists and Moderates* (New York: Oxford University Press, 1991), pp. 162–80.

19. H. Richard Niebuhr, *Christ and Culture* (New York: Harper, 1951).

20. For responses to Niebuhr from Anabaptist writers, see Charles Scriven, *The Transformation of Culture* (Scottdale, Pa.: Herald Press, 1988); John Howard Yoder, *The Priestly Kingdom* (Notre Dame: University of Notre Dame Press, 1988).

21. David Bebbington, *Evangelicalism in Modern Britain: A History from the 1730s to the 1980s* (London: Hyman, 1989), p. 227.

22. David Bebbington, "Baptists and Fundamentalism in Inter-War Britain," in K. Robbins (ed.), *Protestant Evangelicalism: Britain, Ireland, Germany and America, c. 1750 – c. 1950* (Oxford: Ecclesiastical History Society, 1990), pp. 297–326.

23. See G. A. Rawlyk, *Champions of the Truth: Fundamentalism, Modernism and the Maritime Baptists* (Montreal/Kingston: McGill-Queens University Press, 1990); John G. Stackhouse Jr., "The Emergence of a Fellowship: Canadian Evangelicalism in the Twentieth Century," *Church History* 60 (1991): 247–62.

24. Stuart Piggin, "Towards a Bicentennial History of Australian Evangelicalism," *Journal of Religious History* 15 (1988): 20–36.

25. Carl F. H. Henry, *The Uneasy Conscience of Modern Fundamentalism* (Grand Rapids: Eerdmans, 1947).

26. Millard J. Erickson, *The New Evangelical Theology* (Westwood, NJ: Revell, 1968), pp. 22–30.

27. Harold J. Ockenga, "From Fundamentalism, Through New Evangelicalism, to Evangelicalism," in K. S. Kantzer (ed.), *Evangelical Roots* (Nashville: Nelson, 1978), pp. 35–48. The term "new evangelicalism" seems to have its origins in Ockenga's 1947

convocation address to Fuller Theological Seminary. It was popularized by Carl Henry early in 1948, especially in a series of articles in the influential journal *Christian Life and Times*. See Carl F. H. Henry, "The Vigor of the New Evangelicalism," *Christian Life and Times*, January 1948, 30–32; March 1948, 35–38; 85; April 1948, 32–35; 65–69.

28. James Barr, *Fundamentalism* (London: SCM Press, 1977). For an example of the criticisms now being levelled against Barr's uncritical use of the category of "literal sense," see Paul R. Noble, "The *Sensus Literalis*: Jowett, Childs and Barr," *Journal of Theological Studies* 44 (1993: 1–23. A major critique of Barr's work, currently in preparation by Harriet Rawson (New College, Oxford), promises to advance our understanding of the nature of Fundamentalism in England.

29. Clark Pinnock, "Defining American Fundamentalism: A Response," in N. J. Cohen (ed.), *The Fundamentalist Phenomenon* (Grand Rapids: Eerdmans, 1990), pp. 38–55; quotes at pp. 40–41.

30. Richard Quebedeaux, *The Young Evangelicals* (New York: Harper & Row, 1974), p. 19.

31. Stephen W. Sykes, *The Identity of Christianity* (London: SPCK, 1984), pp. 102–18; idem, "The Fundamentals of Christianity," in S. Sykes and J. Booty (eds.), *The Study of Anglicanism* (Philadelphia: Fortress Press, 1988), pp. 231–45.

32. John Macquarrie, *Jesus Christ in Modern Thought* (London: SCM Press, 1990), p. 253.

33. S. W. Sykes, *The Integrity of Anglicanism* (London: Mowbray, 1978), p. 32.

34. Sykes, *The Integrity of Anglicanism*, p. 32.

35. John Macquarrie, "The Anglican Theological Tradition," in *Theology, Church and Ministry* (London: SCM Press, 1986), pp. 91–104; quote at pp. 99–100.

36. Cited F. W. Knickerbocker, *Free Minds: John Morley and His Friends* (Cambridge, Mass.: Harvard University Press, 1943), p. 163. On Victorian liberalism in general, see Ian Bradley, *The Optimists: Themes and Personalities in Victorian Liberalism* (London: Faber & Faber, 1980).

37. J. F. Bethune-Baker, *The Faith of the Apostles Creed: An Essay in Adjustment of Belief and Faith* (London: Macmillan, 1918).

38. George Tyrrell, *Christianity at the Cross-Roads* (1909; repr. London: Black, 1963), p. 49.

39. See William A. Galston, *Liberal Purposes: Goods, Virtues and Diversity in the Liberal State* (Cambridge: Cambridge University Press, 1990).

40. Peter L. Berger, *A Far Glory: The Quest for Faith in an Age of Credulity* (New York: Free Press, 1992), pp. 9–10.

41. Eugene B. Borowitz, "The Enduring Truth of Religious Liberalism," in N. J. Cohen (ed.), *The Fundamentalist Phenomenon* (Grand Rapids: Eerdmans, 1990), pp. 230–47; quote at p. 231.

42. The subject is fascinating and well worth an excursion by the interested reader. The older view that Hooker drew heavily upon Thomist notions, found in Alessandro P. D"Entrève, *Riccardo Hooker: contributo alla teoria e alla storia del diritto naturale* (Turin: University of Turin, 1932), has now been modified. See W. J. Torrance Kirby, *Richard Hooker's Doctrine of the Royal Supremacy* (Leiden: E. J. Brill, 1990); Joan Lockwood O'Donovan, *Theology of Law and Authority in the English Reformation* (Atlanta, Ga.: Scholars Press, 1991).

43. See A. Plantinga and N. Wolterstorff (eds.), *Faith and Rationality: Reason and Belief in God* (Notre Dame: University of Notre Dame, 1983).

44. Berger, *A Far Glory*, pp. 10–11.

45. Berger, *A Far Glory*, p. 12 (emphasis in original).

46. Jacques Ellul, *Violence* (New York: Seabury Press, 1969), p. 28.

47. Wade Clark Roof and William McKinney, *American Mainline Religion: Its Changing Shape and Future* (Brunswick, N.J.: Rutgers University Press, 1987).

48. Roof and McKinney, *American Mainline Religion*, p. 242.

49. John Habgood, *Confessions of a Conservative Liberal* (London: SPCK, 1988).

50. John Habgood, "Reflections on the Liberal Position," in D.

W. Hardy and P. H. Sedgewick (eds.), *The Weight of Glory: A Vision and Practice for Christian Faith* (Edinburgh: T & T Clark, 1991), pp. 5–14.

51. Habgood, "Reflections on the Liberal Position," p. 9.

52. Adrian Hastings, *A History of English Christianity 1920–1985* (London: Collins, 1986), pp. 662–63.

53. For what follows, see the masterful survey, richly furnished with primary source references, in Bradley J. Longfield, *The Presbyterian Controversy: Fundamentalists, Modernists and Moderates* (New York: Oxford University Press, 1991).

54. W. Norman Pittenger, *The Episcopalian Way of Life* (Englewood Cliffs, N.J.: Prentice-Hall, 1957), p. 13.

55. John Booty, *The Episcopal Church in Crisis* (Cambridge, Mass.: Cowley, 1988); Stephen Sykes, *The Integrity of Anglicanism* (London: Mowbrays, 1978) offer perceptive comments, focusing on the American and English scenes respectively. The "Baltimore Declaration" (26 May 1991) is a reaction against what its parish-based authors perceive to be an excessive inclusivism within the Episcopal Church: see E. Radner and G. R. Sumner (eds.), *Reclaiming Faith: Essays on Orthodoxy in the Episcopal Church and the Baltimore Declaration* (Grand Rapids: Eerdmans, 1993). There are interesting parallels between this document and the earlier "Hartford Appeal" (1975): see *Against the World for the World* (New York: Seabury, 1976).

56. See Alan M. G. Stephenson, *The Rise and Decline of English Modernism* (London: SPCK, 1984). On the United States, see William R. Hutchison, *The Modernist Impulse in American Protestantism* (New York: Oxford University Press, 1982).

57. Hastings Rashdall, *The Idea of Atonement in Christian Theology* (London: Macmillan, 1919). For criticism and evaluation, see Alister E. McGrath, "The Moral Theory of the Atonement. An Historical and Theological Critique," *Scottish Journal of Theology* 38 (1985): 205–20.

58. Adrian Hastings, *A History of English Christianity 1920–1985* (London: Collins, 1986), p. 261.

59. Hans Küng, "Against Contemporary Roman Catholic

Fundamentalism," in H. Küng and J. Moltmann (eds), *Fundamentalism as an Ecumenical Challenge* Concilium 1992/3 (London: SCM Press, 1992), pp. 116–25; quote at p. 124.

60. See George Hunsinger, "Hans Frei as a Theologian: The Quest for a Generous Orthodoxy," *Modern Theology* 8 (1992): 103–28.

61. See Alister E. McGrath, "Why Doctrine? The Confession of a Disillusioned Liberal," in G. Kuhrt (ed.), *Doctrine Matters* (London: Hodder & Stoughton, 1993), pp. 1–18.

62. The most important works relating to this development include: Hans W. Frei, *The Eclipse of Biblical Narrative* (New Haven: Yale University Press, 1974); George A. Lindbeck, *The Nature of Doctrine: Religion and Theology in a Postliberal Age* (Philadelphia: Fortress Press, 1984); William C. Placher, *Unapologetic Theology: A Christian Voice in a Pluralistic Conversation* (Louisville: Westminster/John Knox Press, 1989); R. E. Thiemann, *Revelation and Theology: The Gospel as Narrated Promise* (Notre Dame: University of Notre Dame, 1985).

63. Lindbeck, *Nature of Doctrine*, pp. 32–41.

64. David Tracy, "On Naming the Present," in P. Hillyer (ed.), *On the Threshold of the Third Millennium* Concilium 1990/1 (London: SCM Press, 1990), pp. 66–85; quotes at p. 75.

65. Alister E. McGrath, *The Genesis of Doctrine* (Oxford/Cambridge, Mass.: Blackwell, 1990), pp. 14–80.

Chapter 6

1. Roberto Weiss, *The Renaissance Discovery of Classical Antiquity* (Oxford: Blackwell, 1988).

2. A point stressed by Jaroslav Pelikan, *The Vindication of Tradition* (New Haven: Yale University Press, 1984).

3. See the suggestive study of Aidan Nichols, "T. S. Eliot and Yves Congar on the Nature of Tradition," *Angelicum* 61 (1984): 473–85, which shows how "tradition" and "originality" are mutually linked.

4. For analysis and comment, see Alister E. McGrath, *The*

Genesis of Doctrine (Oxford/Cambridge, Mass.: Blackwell, 1990), pp. 165–71.

5. David Tracy, "On Naming the Present," in P. Hillyer (ed.), *On the Threshold of the Third Millennium* Concilium 1990/1 (London: SCM Press, 1990), pp. 66–85; quote at p. 75.

6. John H. Crook, *Evolution of Human Consciousness* (Oxford: Oxford University Press, 1980), p. 361.

7. See Phyllis D. Airhart, *Serving the Present Age: Revivalism, Progressivism and the Methodist Tradition in Canada* (Montreal: McGill-Queen's University Press, 1992).

8. See the Oxford D.Phil. thesis of Martie Davie, "A Study in the Development of British Quaker Theology since 1895 with Special Reference to Janet Scott's 1980 Swarthmore Lecture."

9. Timothy George and David S. Dockery, *Baptist Theologians* (Nashville, Tenn.: Boardman, 1990), p. 14.

10. Wade Clark Roof and William McKinney, *American Mainline Religion: Its Changing Shape and Future* (New Brunswick, N.J.: Rutgers University Press, 1987), p. 241.

11. Stanley Hauerwas and William H. Willimon, *Resident Aliens: Life in the Christian Colony* (Nashville: Abingdon Press, 1989), p. 18.

12. Robert Morgan (ed.), "Preface," in *The Religion of the Incarnation: Anglican Essays in Commemoration of Lux Mundi* (Bristol: Bristol Classical Press, 1989), p. xi.

13. For a careful study of the issues, see Anthony C. Thiselton, "Academic Freedom, Religious Tradition and the Morality of Christian Scholarship," in M. Santer (ed.), *Their Lord and Ours* (London: SPCK, 1982), pp. 20–45.

15. H. Richard Niebuhr, *Christ and Culture* (New York: Harper, 1951). For criticisms, see John Howard Yoder, *The Priestly Kingdom* (Notre Dame: University of Notre Dame Press, 1988); idem, "A People in the World," in J. L. Garrett (ed.), *The Concept of the Believer's Church* (Scottdale, Pa.: Herald Press, 1969), pp. 252–83; Hauerwas and Willimon, *Resident Aliens: Life in the Christian Colony*, pp. 39–43.

16. See Lesslie Newbigin, *Foolishness to the Greeks: The*

Gospel and Western Culture (Geneva: WCC, 1986).

17. Richard John Neuhaus, *The Naked Public Square: Religion and Democracy in America* 2d ed. (Grand Rapids: Eerdmans, 1986).

18. See the disquieting analysis of Robert P. Ericksen, *Theologians Under Hitler: Gerhard Kittel, Paul Althaus and Emanuel Hirsch* (New Haven: Yale University Press, 1985). The case of Emanuel Hirsch (1888–1972), who openly supported the Nazis, is especially significant.

19. Hauerwas and Willimon, *Resident Aliens: Life in the Christian Colony*, pp. 24–25.

20. See Ian Breward, *Australia: The Most Godless Place under Heaven?* (Melbourne: Beacon Hill, 1988).

21. See Robert J. Schreiter, *Constructing Local Theologies* (Maryknoll, N.Y.: Orbis, 1986).

Chapter 7

1. See Anthony Russell, *The Clerical Profession* (London: SPCK, 1984) for an analysis of the increasing professionalization of the clergy and the search for clerical "distinctiveness."

2. Richard John Neuhaus, in *First Things*, October 1991, p. 71.

3. David Lodge, *Nice Work* (London: Penguin, 1989); idem, *Small World: An Academic Romance* (London: Secker & Warburg, 1984).

4. Basil Mitchell, *How to Play Theological Ping–Pong* (London: Hodder & Stoughton, 1990), p. 34.

5. Adrian Hastings, *A History of English Christianity 1920–1985* (London: Collins, 1986), pp. 662–63.

6. The impact of Allan Bloom's *The Closing of the American Mind* (New York: Simon & Schuster, 1987) should be noted here.

7. See Paul V. Mankowski S.J., "Academic Religion," in *First Things* (May 1992): 31–37; quote at p. 34.

8. See Alberto Caracciolo, *La città futura: saggi sulla figura*

e il pensiero di Antonio Gramsci (Milan: Feltrinelli, 1976); Giuseppe Fiori, *Vita di Antonio Gramsci* (Bari: Editori Laterza, 1989).

9. For some perceptive observations on the dangers associated with "authority," see Paul Avis, *Authority, Leadership and Conflict in the Church* (London: Geoffrey Chapman Mowbray, 1992).

10. But see the important discussion by John Macquarrie, "The Bishop and the Theologian," in *Theology, Church and Ministry* (London: SCM Press, 1986), pp. 179–87.

11. *Theological Freedom and Social Responsibility* (New York: Seabury Press, 1967), p. 32.

12. Edward Farley, *Theologia: The Fragmentation and Unity of Theological Education* (Philadelphia: Fortress Press, 1983), pp. x, 7. The debate that resulted may be followed in works such as J. C. Hough and J. B. Cobb, Jr. (eds.), *Christian Identity and Theological Education* (Chico, Calif.: Scholar's Press, 1985); Charles M. Wood, *Vision and Discernment: An Orientation in Theological Study* (Atlanta: Scholar's Press, 1985); Edward Farley, *The Fragility of Knowledge: Theological Education in the Church and University* (Philadelphia: Fortress Press, 1988).

13. On Calvin's understanding of the dialectic between theology and experience, see Wilhelm Balke, "The Word of God and *Experientia* according to Calvin," in W. H. Neuser (ed.), *Calvinus Ecclesiae Doctor* (Kampen: Kok, 1978), pp. 19–31.

14. Søren Kierkegaard, *Unscientific Postscript* (London: Oxford University Press, 1941), pp. 169–224. Cf. P. L. Holmer, "Kierkegaard and Religious Propositions," *Journal of Religion* 35 (1955): 135–46.

15. According to David Lowes Watson, "Spiritual Formation in Ministry Training," *Christian Century* 101 (6–13 February, 1991): 122–4.

16. See Walter L. Liefield and Linda M. Cannell, "Spiritual Formation and Theological Education," in J. I. Packer and L. Wilkinson (eds.), *Alive to God: Studies in Spirituality* (Downers Grove, Ill.: Inter-Varsity, 1992), pp. 239–52.

17. Owen Chadwick, "Indifference and Morality," in P. N.

Brooks (ed.), *Christian Spirituality: Essays in Honour of Gordon Rupp* (London: SCM Press, 1975), pp. 203–30.

18. Thus there is no entry on "spirituality" in D. McKim (ed.), *Encyclopaedia of the Reformed Faith* (Lousville: Westminster/John Knox Press, 1992); the material relating to this theme is to be found under the entry "piety" (pp. 278–79).

19. Thomas C. Oden, *Pastoral Theology: Essentials of Ministry* (San Francisco: Harper & Row, 1983), p. 311.

20. Adrian Hastings, *A History of English Christianity 1920–1985* (London: Collins, 1986), pp. 662–63.

21. Geoffrey Wainwright, *Doxology: The Praise of God in Worship, Doctrine and Life* (New York: Oxford University Press, 1980). For a more recent discussion, see Aidan Kavanagh, *On Liturgical Theology* (New York: Pueblo, 1984). The formula *lex orandi, lex credendi* has made a significant impact recently within Episcopalian circles, as can be seen from both L. L. Mitchell, *Prayer Shapes Believing: A Theological Commentary on the Book of Common Prayer* (Wilton, Conn.: Morehouse, 1985) and the appearance of the Latin tag on the front cover of the *Anglican Theological Review* in recent years.

22. James I. Packer, "An Introduction to Systematic Spirituality," *Crux* 26/1 (March 1990): 2–8; quote at p. 6.

23. See the perceptive comments of Mark Schwehn, *Exiles from Eden: Religion and the Academic Vocation in America* (New York: Oxford University Press, 1993), pp. 56–57.

Index